GLASS &
METALWARE

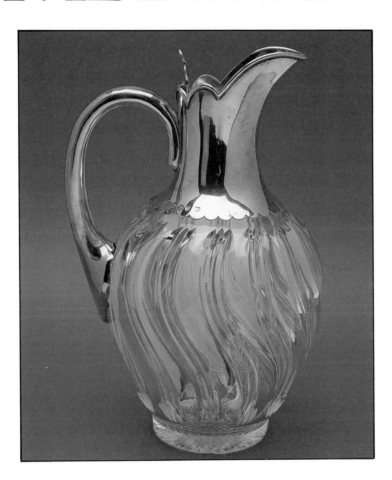

COLLECTING
FOR PLEASURE

GLASS &
METALWARE

BRACKEN BOOKS

Editor Dorothea Hall
Art Editor Gordon Robertson
Production Inger Faulkner

Concept, design and production by
Marshall Cavendish Books
119 Wardour Street
London W1V 3TD

This edition published 1992 by Bracken Books
an imprint of Studio Editions Limited,
Princess House, 50 Eastcastle Street
London W1N 7AP England

Typeset by Litho Link Ltd.
Printed and bound in Hong Kong

ISBN 1 85170 915 0

Some of this material was previously published in the Marshall Cavendish partwork *Times Past*

CONTENTS

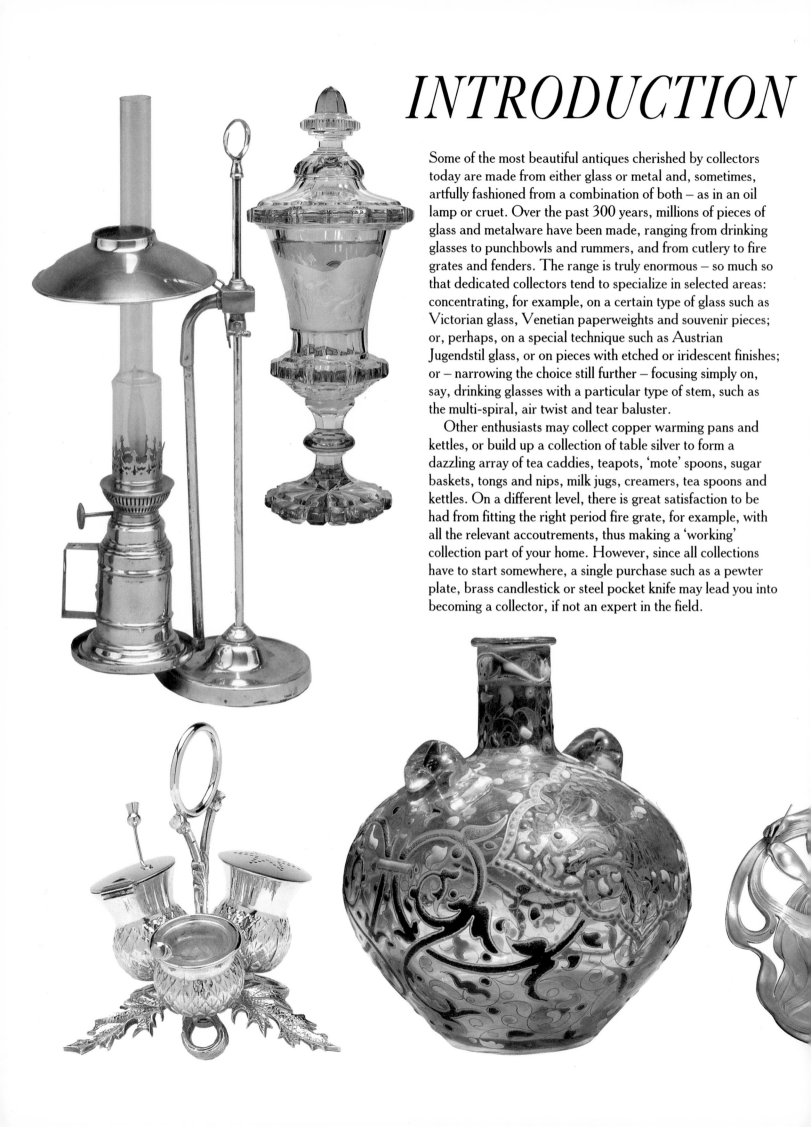

INTRODUCTION

Some of the most beautiful antiques cherished by collectors today are made from either glass or metal and, sometimes, artfully fashioned from a combination of both – as in an oil lamp or cruet. Over the past 300 years, millions of pieces of glass and metalware have been made, ranging from drinking glasses to punchbowls and rummers, and from cutlery to fire grates and fenders. The range is truly enormous – so much so that dedicated collectors tend to specialize in selected areas: concentrating, for example, on a certain type of glass such as Victorian glass, Venetian paperweights and souvenir pieces; or, perhaps, on a special technique such as Austrian Jugendstil glass, or on pieces with etched or iridescent finishes; or – narrowing the choice still further – focusing simply on, say, drinking glasses with a particular type of stem, such as the multi-spiral, air twist and tear baluster.

Other enthusiasts may collect copper warming pans and kettles, or build up a collection of table silver to form a dazzling array of tea caddies, teapots, 'mote' spoons, sugar baskets, tongs and nips, milk jugs, creamers, tea spoons and kettles. On a different level, there is great satisfaction to be had from fitting the right period fire grate, for example, with all the relevant accoutrements, thus making a 'working' collection part of your home. However, since all collections have to start somewhere, a single purchase such as a pewter plate, brass candlestick or steel pocket knife may lead you into becoming a collector, if not an expert in the field.

This fascinating, fully illustrated book covers all these aspects admirably. From Georgian times through to the Art Deco 1930s, it illustrates the abundant choice of glass and metalware collectables that are still widely available today. The scholarly and informative text discusses each item in detail and, in the process, gives the reader insight into the lifestyles and fashions of the past. Much useful advice is given on what the collector should look for in an antique, how to assess quality and craftsmanship, identify makers' marks, and distinguish between the real and the not so real. In addition, price guides accompany each item discussed to help in calculating a sensible purchase price. However, do remember that prices can vary across the country, and that rarity and the particular condition of a piece remain important considerations. (See the Price Guide below for the key to the price codes used within the book.)

I am confident that this beautifully produced volume will arouse your interest in antiques and, perhaps, help you to create a collection that will be both a sound investment and a lasting joy.

Tony Curtis

PRICE GUIDE

KEY		❺ £200-£400
❶ £15-£30		❻ £400-£750
❷ £30-£60		❼ £750-£1500
❸ £60-£100		❽ £1500-£6000
❹ £100-£200		❾ £6,000 plus

The Punchbowl

Once part of the rowdy drinking rituals of the Georgian Gentleman, the punchbowl eventually took its place in the polite drawing rooms of Regency England

T he word 'punch,' which may have derived from the Hindustani 'panchi', meaning five (the number of ingredients traditionally used to make the drink), or 'puncheon' (an enormous cask used to transport rum), entered common speech in the mid-17th century. This was no doubt testimony to the rapid assimilation of the beverage by a society which (if the 18th-century engravings of William Hogarth are anything to go by) was marked by an inordinate love of the bottle.

At that date, punch was a masculine, convivial drink, enjoyed by its afficionados both at home and in the tavern. Hogarth's engraving 'A Midnight Modern Conversation' presents a typical all-night punch-drinking session, and James Boswell reported a 'severe headach' on the morning of 26 September 1785 as the aftermath of a similar occasion during his tour of the Hebrides with Dr Johnson.

In the mid-18th century, such riotous bouts would have been reserved for male gatherings in the dining room or the private rooms used by the man of the house, but towards the Regency era changing manners and morals brought punch into polite society. Balls and assemblies developed as a feature of 'genteel' life, and punch was served in the saloon or drawing room where these took place.

Chinese Punchbowl

THIS CHINESE PORCELAIN PUNCHBOWL IS TYPICAL OF THE MANY THAT WERE EXPORTED TO EUROPE IN THE 18TH CENTURY. THE EXTERIOR IS DECORATED WITH FIGURE SCENES AND THE INTERIOR WITH FISH.

Punch, like tea, owed its existence to the opening of trading connections with the Indies. Of its five ingredients, sugar came from plantations in the West Indies and spices from the East; others were spirits, water and citrus fruit. The basic punch recipe was open to infinite variation and individual recipes were often kept secret. Rum vied with brandy (the former was particularly popular in Scotland), tea could replace water, and milk could be added to make milk

▲ *Sir Bourchier Wray is depicted ladling out punch in the cabin of a ship, which is leaning dangerously to port. His punchbowl is inscribed with a Latin motto 'Dulce est Desipere in Loco' (it is sweet to play the fool).*

punch. The resulting concoction could be drunk hot or cold.

Punch drinking involved a certain amount of ceremony, which was presided over by a host or chairman. The equipment used for the ritual included the punchbowl or jorum, the monteith, the spice box, the nutmeg grater, the punch pot, glasses or 'rummers,' the punch strainer, the ladle, whisk and toddy lifter.

Punchbowls were made in ceramic, silver, glass and even wood – a reflection of the fact that punch was drunk by people of different social classes and incomes. The earliest identifiable silver example dates from 1680. Today silver bowls are comparatively rare, production having ceased around the 1820s (though copies of Georgian styles appear in the Victorian era) and they consequently fetch rather high prices.

THE MONTEITH

The monteith, first recorded in the diary of Anthony Wood in 1683, was 'a vessel or bason notched at the brim to let drinking vessels hang there by the foot, so that the body or drinking place might hang in the water to cool them.' It was named after 'a fantasticall Scott named "Monsieur Monteigh" who . . . . wore the bottome of his cloake or coat so notched.' By 1690 the rim had become detachable, so that it could be lifted off and the monteith could serve both as glass cooler and punch bowl.

The scalloped or notched rim of the monteith was picked out with foliage or was elaborately scrolled and decorated with masks or shells and usually accompanied with lion's mask, drop ring handles on a fluted body; the punchbowl, however, was usually plainer. Like the monteith, it often bore a coat of arms, sometimes enclosed within a cartouche, and it very rarely came with a cover.

Monteiths declined in popularity after 1720, while punchbowls became more widespread, and more elaborate in design. They came in a number of styles ranging from the circular to the bombé (swollen) shape which became popular towards the end of the century, and most had a stepped moulded foot. Silver punchbowls were also used for presentation purposes and engraved accordingly.

CERAMIC PUNCHBOWLS

Ceramic punchbowls, produced in most kinds of pottery and porcelain including creamware and pearlware, enjoyed a constant popularity. Some porcelain examples were imported from Canton in

▶ *This impressive delftware punchbowl was made in Bristol in 1743 and painted by Joseph Fowler. The exterior shows scenes from songs by George Bickham and the interior shows a punchbowl on a table surrounded by chairs.*

AN IRISH GLASS PUNCHBOWL DATING FROM AROUND 1820, WITH DELICATELY CUT DECORATION SET WITHIN OVALS.

REGENCY MASON'S IRONSTONE PUNCHBOWL WITH VERY RARE IMARI DECORATION INSPIRED BY JAPANESE PATTERNS.

AN ORNATE SILVER PUNCHBOWL DECORATED WITH SCROLLS, LEAVES AND FLOWERS, WITH A CARTOUCHE FOR A FAMILY CREST.

Glass and Metalware

the second half of the 18th century, and these were often decorated with hunting scenes.

For those who could not afford oriental porcelain, there were cheaper earthenware pieces with tin glaze, known as delftware. They usually bore blue designs on cream slip, often showing sailing boats and harbours. Delftware was produced in England from the late 16th century in imitation of Dutch Delft pottery; the factories in Lambeth and Bristol manufactured the most notable examples. Designs, which were painted outside and inside the bowl, sometimes included the name of the owner, a motto or some political slogan; punch was the favourite drink of the Whig party in Georgian times. Punchbowls can also be found in stoneware; the brown salt-glazed lathe-turned stoneware made in Nottingham in the 18th century was of very high quality. Designs were incised with a sharp instrument before the bowl was fired.

PUNCH POTS

An alternative to the punchbowl was the punch pot. Like a giant teapot, but without the spout strainer, the punch pot was made in white salt-glazed stoneware or fortified soft-paste soapstone. The handle, spout and lid finial were often of crabstock design. Wedgwood also made punch pots in earthenware with a coloured glaze, creamware, black basaltes and 'rosso antico'. Punch kettles in lathe-turned red stoneware were manufactured from the late 1760s through to the 19th century.

Glass punchbowls first appeared in the mid-18th century but only became really popular in the Regency period. The earliest examples were generally circular with a domed foot, similar to contemporary metal and ceramic types. There are a few early examples of glass monteiths, but these were soon superseded by simpler glass coolers which held

▲ Hogarth's 'A Midnight Modern Conversation' is a humorous portrayal of the dire effects of excessive punch drinking. Some members of the party are growing quarrelsome while others doze; one man has even fallen off his chair losing his wig in the process.

◄ *Glass punchbowl from about 1810, with a beautifully cut pattern of flowers and stems.*

PRICE GUIDE **6**

▼◄ *An ogee-shaped rummer with petal moulding, decorated with engraved swags. It dates from 1790.*

PRICE GUIDE **4**

▼ *Bucket-shaped rummer with a band of engraved leaves and spirals around the rim, and a knopped stem.*

PRICE GUIDE **4**

◄ *An Irish silver and horn punch ladle with a coin set in the bowl, dating from around 1720.*

PRICE GUIDE **5**

▲ *A Chamberlain's Worcester punchbowl from 1820, with attractive decoration of leaves and flowers.*

PRICE GUIDE **7**

▲ *Joseph Highmore's portrait of Mr Oldham and his guests presents a fairly decorous gathering, but decanter, punchbowl and clay pipes – important aids to conviviality – are all included.*

▼▶ *Cup-shaped undecorated late Georgian rummer with a solid-looking stepped foot.*

PRICE GUIDE **4**

▼ *Plain and functional bucket-shaped rummer from 1790, with an annular knop stem.*

PRICE GUIDE **4**

bowls, of Sheffield plate (ceramic versions are also known), were finely pierced with two cast handles of a size that could fit over the circumference of a punch bowl. Decoratively perforated flat plate rests gave way to cast scrolled handles or plain drawn silver wire, but the bowl was always of sufficient size to allow a small squeezed orange to soak into the punch.

The punch was served from the bowl with a punch ladle or toddy lifter. Before 1700, the punch ladle was plain with a wooden or tubular silver handle set at a 45° angle to the bowl of the ladle, which was made of silver or pewter. By 1740 bowls had become oval with a single lip and fluted. Handles were made of ebony, ivory, walnut or whalebone. The Adam period saw a return to simpler styles. The oval bowl often had an old silver coin set in a decorative rim. Smaller versions, known as toddy ladles, were made in Scotland. The warming restorative toddy, made from sugar, boiling water and whisky, was also served from the punch bowl. Toddy lifters or fillers looked like slim versions of the decanter. They had a quarter pint capacity, an elongated neck with a small hole and another larger one at the base. The lifter was plunged into the punch until full, when the thumb was pressed over the neck aperture. It was then held over the drinking glass and the punch released. Lifters became popular around 1780 and eventually superseded the ladle.

only one or two glasses. By 1780 glass punchbowls had become brilliantly cut and engraved following Anglo-Irish styles.

They were often accompanied by a matching ladle and set of drinking glasses, initially with a baluster stem, but by 1800 small thick cups with handles had become fashionable. Larger glasses, known as toddy rummers, were produced with circular and very occasionally square bases. These were short stemmed with a bucket-shaped bowl which was often engraved with sporting scenes or the insignia of a society or club.

ORANGES AND LEMONS
The 'spiritous liquor', as Pepys called it, was flavoured with an orange or lemon. Orange or lemon strainers made of silver and later, like the punch-

▲ *Late 18th-century delftware punchbowl made in England but decorated with Chinese scenes.*

PRICE GUIDE **5**

▶ *A pleasingly simple glass punchbowl from 1810, with a band of diamond-cut decoration.*

PRICE GUIDE **6**

Georgian Drinking Glasses

Despite their fragility, hand-blown Georgian drinking glasses with their delicate engraving and tastefully twisted stems are still available at surprisingly reasonable prices

Georgian drinking glasses are but one expression of 18th-century English technical and artistic achievement. Their relative weight and thickness, and the peculiar gleam of the glass itself are innate characteristics of these beautiful vessels. But it is also their great variety of shapes – suitable for supping the various beverages and distillations of the period – together with their delicate engraving and fascinating decorated stems, which makes them prized as objects of beauty.

Despite the apparent fragility of glassware, Georgian drinking glasses have survived in great enough numbers to be avidly collected today. Although some are rare and therefore expensive, many beautiful and interesting examples can still be acquired for quite reasonable sums.

THE HISTORY OF GLASSES

Before about 1675, drinking glasses and glassware of any kind were expensive and exclusive luxuries. In refined and wealthy circles, wine, ale, spirits and cordials were supped from delicate, finely blown glasses that had either been imported from Venice or made in Europe by Italian craftsmen.

These early drinking glasses were made of soda glass. This was a mixture of soda and silica, and the glassware that resulted had a slightly dirty tinge. Italy controlled the monopoly for its manufacture.

GEORGE RAVENSCROFT

From the late 18th century, however, England began to rival Italy as an important centre of glass-making. In 1674, George Ravenscroft, an English glass-maker, had patented a new kind of glass. This was known as lead glass, and contained both lead and silica. By comparison to soda glass, it was marvellously clear. It was also less brittle, enabling it to survive engraving without easily fracturing. Glass-making skills rapidly developed and by the end of the 17th century 27 glasshouses existed.

Like all glassware made before about 1825, early

drinking glasses were hand-blown. They were made in three separate parts – the bowl, the stem and the foot. First the bowl was attached to the stem, and then the foot was added.

The typical early 18th-century drinking glass, known as a baluster, had a conical or funnel-shaped bowl, a short, baluster-shaped stem with a pronounced swelling, or knop, and a flat, domed or conical foot. As the 18th century progressed, the early balusters evolved into lighter forms, with longer, finer stems and smaller knops. Bowls also assumed a wider variety of shapes, and engraving, gilding and enamelling were used for decoration.

While the knopped stem, in its many forms, continued to be exploited to the full, the contrasting long, plain, unknopped stem became a feature of a range of elegant drinking glasses.

The old practice of enclosing a bubble of air in the stem also evolved into the more complex air-twist stem. This was achieved by trapping a bubble of air in the molten glass for the stem and twisting it, resulting in the delicate swirling patterns. Later, similar effects were produced with rods of opaque white and coloured glass. The stems of glasses decorated in this way are termed 'opaque-twist' and 'colour-twist' respectively.

Alcoholic drinks of the Georgian period included strong ale, cider, wine, cordials and ratafia (a kernel-flavoured liqueur), most of which involved special glasses. Strong, potent ale was sipped in modest quantities from glasses with slim, elongated bowls. Fittingly, the bowl was sometimes engraved with a motif of hops and barley. Later in the 18th century, the hops and barley motif also decorated tumblers, large goblets known as rummers, and other glasses for ale. Glasses with slender, elongated bowls were also suitable for cider or champagne.

SHAPES AND STYLES

Wine glasses also took a variety of shapes. Bowls were mostly trumpet, bell or rounded funnel shaped. A range of motifs besides the appropriate fruiting vine decorated the bowls of wine glasses. Cordial glasses are distinguishable by their small funnel-shaped or ovoid bowls and tall thick stems. Ratafia glasses, also known as flute cordials, had a slender flute-shaped bowl on a tall thick stem. Not only were the bowls of cordial and ratafia glasses beautifully engraved, many also stood on fine air-twist or colour-twist stems.

Toasting glasses resembled cordial glasses, but the characteristically thick walls of the bowl purposely reduced their capacity. This allowed a toastmaster to remain sober while officiating at social occasions. The toasting glasses used by the assembled company were, by contrast, exceedingly delicate. They generally took the form of undecorated slender flutes. The toast duly drunk, custom dictated that the glass be broken between the fingers. This rather wasteful

◀ *This selection of Georgian glasses shows the enormous variety available to the collector. Note the many shapes and stem styles which include facet-cuts, multi-spiral air- and opaque-twists, as well as central swellings and knops. Elaborate stem styles and rich engravings tend to command high prices.*

practice had been abandoned by approximately 1750.

Sturdiness and solidity were essential to the shape and form of 'firing glasses', if they were to withstand the rough treatment to which they were subjected as merry evenings became merrier. To signal silence before a toast or song, drinkers would rap their glasses loudly on the table; the din that this produced resembled gunfire, hence the term 'firing glass'.

The largest and plainest of Georgian drinking glasses are the rummers. The term is derived from *Römer*, the German word for a goblet. In their typical form they have a large bucket-shaped bowl and a short knopped stem. Many were used in taverns for serving beer, sack, cider and mulled wine. Smaller rummers were used for spirits, such as gin and rum.

METHODS OF DECORATION

Georgian drinking glasses were decorated most commonly by engraving, and more rarely by enamelling or gilding. There were three methods of engraving: scratch engraving, wheel engraving and stipple engraving. Scratch engraving was a straightforward process executed by means of an iron or diamond point. Emblems and other legends were often applied by this means.

◀ *These gentlemen are drinking their wine from flared glasses set on stems with a single ornamental knop. The Georgians had a wide taste in drinks; apart from the many wines, ales and cordials, medicinal waters were also popular. Although these 'medicines' were meant to cure a variety of ailments, most contained alcohol which if nothing else promoted a sense of temporary well-being.*

▶ *A rare and expensive piece, this is an early lead glass by George Ravenscroft. It bears the raven's head seal mark on the stem which he began using in 1677. Before this time, he had had to overcome the problem of crizzling in which an excess of alkali in the glass caused a network of tiny internal cracks to develop, destroying the transparency of the glass.*

▲ *Three 18th-century glasses. From left, a honey-combed moulded goblet on a double series opaque stem; a beer mug c.1760 engraved with hops and barley; and a heavy baluster with a tear, or bubble of air, incorporated into the knop of the stem. Both the goblet and the baluster predate 1780 and probably retain their pointil marks, the rough area on the foot that was later ground away.*

In wheel engraving, which was a speciality of Dutch craftsmen, the glass was held to an abrasive wheel. This method was extensively used for such decoration as hops and barley, fruiting vine, floral borders and elaborate coats of arms.

Stipple engraving was also a Dutch speciality. Built up by clusters of dots, a stipple-engraved image appears to have been literally breathed on to the glass. The effect is faintly ghostly and the decoration all but invisible until the glass is held to the light.

COLLECTORS' TIPS

It is generally safe to assume that the cheaper Georgian drinking glasses on sale today are genuine. Many of the finer types have been faked, however. It is in any case wise to make several checks.

A genuinely antique glass will show slight unevenness and asymmetry that results from hand-blowing. It will also have random scratches and other signs of wear to the base, although this is not too difficult to fake.

Damage renders most Georgian drinking glasses virtually worthless. Chips to the rim or foot can quite easily be ground off, however. A rim or foot that has been ground is angular rather than rounded.

Because drinking glasses are almost never marked, individual manufacturers remain unknown and dating can be only roughly made on the basis of shape and decoration. Small wine glasses should not be mistaken for cordial glasses, which look similar but are more valuable.

·PRICE GUIDE·   GEORGIAN DRINKING GLASSES

Of all Georgian drinking glasses, the cheapest are the plain rummers; later examples are usually priced at £30-£40, or £150 upwards for a set of six. Plain champagne flutes are also good buys at about £30.

Plain-stemmed wine or ale glasses with little or no decoration can usually be bought for £50-£60. Good wheel-engraving, especially in combination with an opaque-twist stem, raises the

price. A wheel-engraved glass is worth about £80-£90. A glass with an opaque-twist stem in addition to good engraving is worth up to about £250-£300. Across the range, considerably higher prices are asked for earlier Georgian examples.

Attractive ratafia and cordial glasses with good engraving and opaque-twist stems command prices in the £300-£450 bracket.

Georgian Drinking Accessories

Among the fascinating array of drinking accessories produced
in the Georgian period were beautifully hand-crafted silver and
glass wares

In the affluent climate of the 18th century, the Georgians already enjoyed a wide range of alcoholic beverages and the flourishing glass and silver industries responded to the demand for fine accessories for the drawing-room and the dining table. Glassware was not nearly so specialized as it is today and, depending on their capacity, most glasses could safely be employed to hold a variety of different drinks.

The well-to-do were fond of good wines at meal times and their potent and sweet cordials which were taken after tea. In addition they enjoyed deliciously spiced hot toddies and punch, not to mention a regular tipple of gin, rum or port. Wines and spirits were not bought in labelled bottles until after 1860 and, in Georgian times, it was customary for householders to take their own bottles to the wine merchant to be filled from wooden casks. Drinks were then poured into clear glass decanters, which showed off their rich, sediment-free colours.

A fine collection of Georgian accessories can be put to loving use and turn a simple pre- or after-dinner drink into a splendid experience.

Silver Service

Finely fashioned silver drinking accessories from the Georgian period offer ample and interesting scope to the collector. The beauty of hand-fashioned silver has long been recognized and the demand for good pieces, together with the value of the metal itself, means that prices can be high even for quite small silver items.

When buying silver, it is best to carry a good hallmark pocket guide as this will enable you to date a piece exactly and immediately to establish the origin and authenticity of a piece. As a general rule, good quality and excellent condition score over rarity in market value terms for silver.

▶ *Silver toddy ladles were used for serving hot, spiced punch. This one has a Queen Anne shilling in its bowl.*

PRICE GUIDE **5**

▶ *This valuable punchbowl was made for the coronation of George IV in 1820. Its elaborate engraved design incorporates the flowers of the union.*

PRICE GUIDE **7**

▼ *Typical early 19th-century silver wine goblet with graceful leaf and bird engraving and characteristic square-plinth foot.*

PRICE GUIDE **6**

▼ *A wooden-handled brandy saucepan which would have been used over a small spirit burner.*

PRICE GUIDE **7**

▼ *Silver wine labels were made for virtually every type of wine and spirit available and the great variety makes them popular collectables.*

PRICE GUIDE **5 6**

▲ *Wine funnels, usually fitted with a strainer, were used for pouring wine into decanters.*

PRICE GUIDE **5 6**

PRICE GUIDE

Georgian Glass

The Georgian period is often called the 'golden age of English glass' – fine workmanship and innovative designs are typical features of its glass ware. Even though huge quantities of glass were being turned out of the factories in the 18th to 19th centuries, until 1825 it was exclusively hand-blown. Understandably, these drinking glasses and decanters have become increasingly popular with collectors.

Georgian glass styles are extremely diverse so many collectors prefer to specialize in one particular area. Glasses with the delicate 'air-twist' or 'opaque-twist' stems in their remarkable spiralled patterns are perennially popular, as is the 18th-century coloured glass first introduced by the glass works in Bristol. Dating antique glass is a skilled exercise, although the swift succession of fashions and particular decorative techniques provide useful clues. Inexperienced collectors should always beware of copies and forgeries – many Georgian styles were deliberately imitated on the continent to satisfy the immense fashion for it abroad.

It is best to avoid buying damaged pieces. Cracks will inevitably cause weakness and chips are not easy to repair successfully. Look out, also, for any defects in the glass itself as they devalue a piece.

◀ Decanters were first used in the early 18th century for pouring wine off sediment in the bottle. Fancy stoppers complemented decorative bodies. Shown from left to right are the faceted lozenge, spire and cut mushroom styles.

PRICE GUIDE ❺

◀ Bristol's famous coloured glass was widely imitated. Dark blue was the most popular followed by dark green, amethyst and, rarest, ruby.

PRICE GUIDE ❸ ❹

PRICE GUIDE

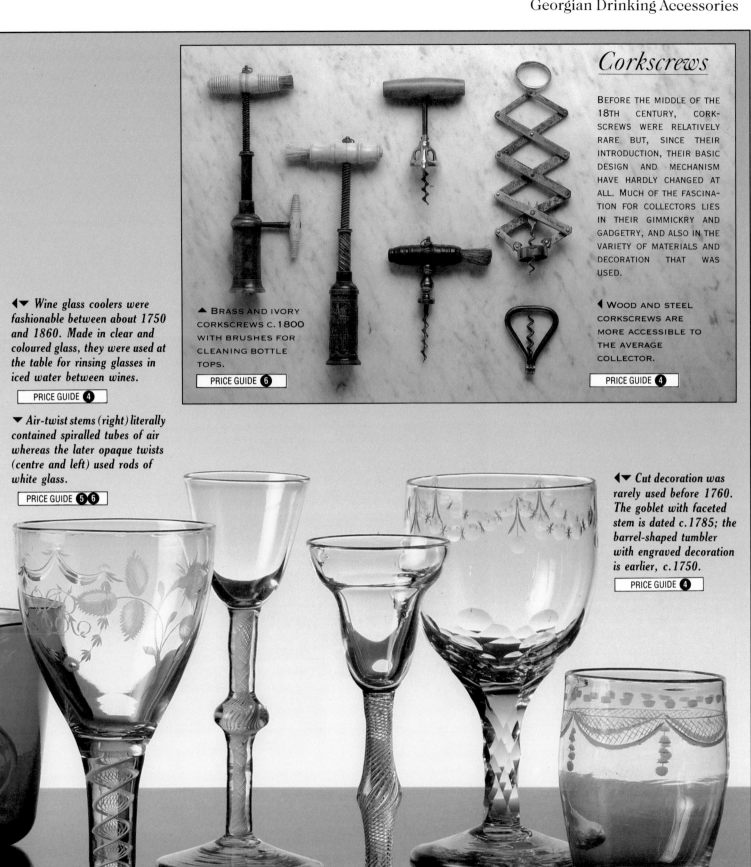

Corkscrews

BEFORE THE MIDDLE OF THE 18TH CENTURY, CORK-SCREWS WERE RELATIVELY RARE BUT, SINCE THEIR INTRODUCTION, THEIR BASIC DESIGN AND MECHANISM HAVE HARDLY CHANGED AT ALL. MUCH OF THE FASCINATION FOR COLLECTORS LIES IN THEIR GIMMICKRY AND GADGETRY, AND ALSO IN THE VARIETY OF MATERIALS AND DECORATION THAT WAS USED.

◀▼ *Wine glass coolers were fashionable between about 1750 and 1860. Made in clear and coloured glass, they were used at the table for rinsing glasses in iced water between wines.*

PRICE GUIDE ❹

▲ BRASS AND IVORY CORKSCREWS C. 1800 WITH BRUSHES FOR CLEANING BOTTLE TOPS.

PRICE GUIDE ❻

◀ WOOD AND STEEL CORKSCREWS ARE MORE ACCESSIBLE TO THE AVERAGE COLLECTOR.

PRICE GUIDE ❹

▼ *Air-twist stems (right) literally contained spiralled tubes of air whereas the later opaque twists (centre and left) used rods of white glass.*

PRICE GUIDE ❺❻

◀▼ *Cut decoration was rarely used before 1760. The goblet with faceted stem is dated c.1785; the barrel-shaped tumbler with engraved decoration is earlier, c.1750.*

PRICE GUIDE ❹

PRICE GUIDE

Victorian Table Glass

As glass became cheaper and more available, the newly affluent
Victorians bought with fervour, and dinner tables throughout
the country sparkled with examples displaying all kinds of
elaborate decoration

The range of table glass available during the Victorian era was spectacular. New techniques perfected by glass manufacturers coupled with the mechanization of the industry led to developments in colour and design which had previously been unthinkable. Colours ranged from deep blues to delicate pinks and the clear glass was cut, etched, engraved or enamelled with glittering results.

DESIGN AND DISTRIBUTION
Rapid increases in international trade in the mid-19th century resulted in the importation of a great variety of glassware and a single table setting often included pieces from Germany, Ireland, Britain and America. The centre of the English glass industry had moved to the Midlands and, by the end of the century, only one factory was still working in London. Many glasshouses were set up around this time, and all struggled to keep up with the demands of an increasingly affluent population. Victorian prosperity fostered a thirst for novelty and the makers continually introduced new methods and ornamental techniques to satisfy demand.

Improvements in communications meant that any design was almost immediately copied and this resulted in an increase in the number of protective patents taken out by manufacturers.

Within the glasshouses there was great competition for skilled workers and men moved frequently, not just between factories

COMPARISONS

Bohemian Glass

BOHEMIAN, OR BIEDERMEIER GLASS WAS ONE OF THE GREATEST INFLUENCES ON THE EUROPEAN GLASS INDUSTRY OF THE 19TH CENTURY. THE BRILLIANT COLOURS AND SUPERB EFFECTS WERE WIDELY COPIED AND MANY BRITISH GLASS FACTORIES WENT ON TO PRODUCE SPECTACULAR GLASS OF THEIR OWN, ONE OF THE MOST POPULAR BEING THE CRANBERRY TYPE.

but to other countries, taking new methods and ideas with them and often making it difficult to establish the origin of particular pieces or sets.

TECHNIQUES AND EFFECTS

Mid-Victorian glass is characterized by the great increase in etched wares. These were delicate but sufficiently ornamental for current taste. Acid etching had been used for some time but it was to be developed on a massive scale in the Stourbridge area.

Outstanding among the developments of the period was the carving away of a thick glass overlay, usually a strong colour such as blue or yellow, to reveal white glass beneath. The skill involved and the time-consuming nature of the process made any pieces in this cameo technique very expensive, although it was, of course, copied, with the cheaper versions acid-etched rather than carved.

The most important advance was the rapid development of press moulding, a technique that was first practised on a large scale in America, where it was originally used in imitation of cut glass. The manufacturers soon became aware of its possibilities and tableware in the form of sphinxes, baskets, people and animals began to appear. Some of these wares carry an impressed mark, the most important British makers being Sowerby and Davidson, both of Gateshead, and Greeners of Sunderland.

The simple clear glass decanters, goblets and tumblers are now lightly considered, enthusiasts preferring the more adventurous experimental items. Slag glass, an opaque glass originally designed to imitate marble, was made by adding slag from local iron foundries. The most common colour was dark purple, reflecting the colour of the slag. Browns, greens and blues were made but these were rarer and more expensive.

CLEAR AND BRILLIANT

Despite the many coloured tablewares, such as vitrified enamel and cranberry, most middle-class households continued to use clear glass for dining. The Victorian wine

▲ *A carved wooden cabinet with glass doors, which is ideal for displaying a collection of varied Victorian drinking glasses.*

◄ *A late 19th century claret jug with an engraved silver top and handle. The wine glasses are part of a set of six.*

▼ *A cameo-cut glass decanter by Emile Gallé, a leading glassmaker and designer in the Art Nouveau style.*

glass had now changed its style. The air twist stem had a more open twist in comparison with the earlier, tightly packed twist; the bowl had increased in size and sometimes seemed out of proportion with the smaller foot (or base). The folded foot, popular in the 18th century, had mostly disappeared – the flatter feet necessitated the removal of the pontil mark; this was the jagged piece of glass remaining where the glass blower had broken the glass off the pontil rod. It was usually ground out, leaving a small, shallow depression. The finest table glass before 1850 was made in Ireland, particularly at Waterford and Cork, where superb decanters, salts, jelly and custard glasses, pickle jars, stands and centrepieces were made by skilled craftsmen. After showing fine work at the Great Exhibition, the Waterford factory closed, as the imposition of an excise duty by the Irish made the glass too expensive in England. The industry was revived in the 1950s after a gap of 100 years, and Waterford glass is still produced in Ireland today.

Because of the design impetus of the 1851 Exhibition and the subsequent developments in coloured and decorated tablewares, there is a tendency to forget that traditional cut glass was still the most popular style. Heavy mitre cutting was common and these bold shapes were sometimes further decorated with engraving. Deep mitre cutting had become viable due to the use of steam-powered machinery. The removal of excise duty on weight led to the very heavy table glass of the 1850s and 60s. Pressed wares were fire-polished to give some brilliance, but genuine cut wine glasses and decanters continued to reign in the dining room.

Jugs and Decanters

Decanters and decanter jugs were first used at table in the early 18th century when it became fashionable to decant wine from casks in order to leave the sediment. The basic shape of the bottles and jugs has changed little since the early days.

For claret, the Victorians preferred to use a claret jug which had a characteristically wider neck, often silver-mounted with a small hinged lid rather than a stopper.

The decoration which the Victorians applied to their bottles and jugs far exceeded that of the table glasses. Cased, flashed, etched, and enamelled work became common after 1850, and wheel engraving made it possible to create claret jugs in Stourbridge with almost complete surface ornamentation.

Though coloured decanters were the most interesting development of the period, cut and pressed clear glass remained most popular with all classes. The most expensive cut decanters were made at Waterford, frequently in sets of three or four for the impressive lockable sideboard stands known as tantalus (designed to prevent servants from helping themselves to the spirits contained within).

◀ A flashed wine decanter with a mushroom stopper, a hooped neck and grape and vineleaf decoration. The clear glass was dipped into molten red glass and the design was then cut out to reveal the clear glass beneath.

PRICE GUIDE **5**

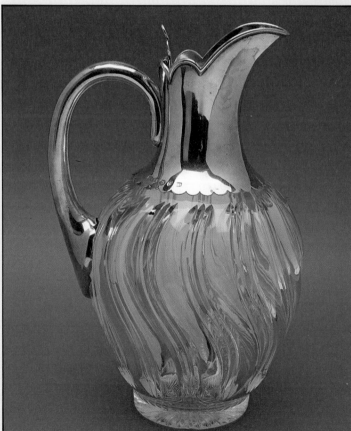

◀ A late Victorian cut-glass claret jug with a hallmarked silver lid. The lid, whose lever is visible, sits within the spout, keeping dust off the wine.

PRICE GUIDE **7**

▶ An attractive example of a cased-glass wine decanter in the shape of a wine bottle. Its glass-topped cork stopper is silver-mounted. White glass has been fused onto the green glass and the vine design has been cut out.

PRICE GUIDE **5**

PRICE GUIDE

▲ A bell-shaped, mould-blown, clear glass decanter with a ground-glass stopper. Mould-blowing, where glass is blown into a mould so that the interior shape matches the exterior shape, dates back to ancient Egypt.

PRICE GUIDE ❹

▶ A wine decanter with a cut-glass neck and engraved vineleaf decorations on the body. The stopper has been mould-blown. The bowl behind is a Bohemian flushed glass tazza, used by the Victorians for sweetmeats.

PRICE GUIDE ❺

PRICE GUIDE

Drinking Glasses

Advances in colouring and design had little effect on middle-class taste. At dinner each person was given a sherry, champagne, claret and water glass for the popular sparkling mineral waters. A water carafe with matching tumblers for plain water was also available. After the cheese, the table was re-set for dessert with wine and finger glasses. Liqueur sets with their etched clear glass enhanced by silver holders were also used.

Etched decoration is most typical of the period, the developments in acid etching making it possible to cover water sets with ornamentation quite cheaply. Grapes and vine leaves usually bordered wine glasses, with hops and barley circling those for ale.

Machine-wheel engraving was another method used to decorate glasses. Similar in process to cutting, the glass is held beneath a rotating wheel which could be changed to give lines of different width. This method needed considerable skill, but gave better results than etching, where the lines were often slightly fuzzy.

▶ A large wine glass designed for drinking red Burgundy. The tall, ovoid bowl rests on a thick, faceted, cut-glass stem and a solid foot. The heaviness of the glass combined with the bowl's low centre of gravity ensures stability.

PRICE GUIDE ❸

▶▶ A thinner, more delicate design of Burgundy glass with a globular bowl on a slim stem above a broad but light foot. The bowl is etched with a series of geometric designs.

PRICE GUIDE ❸

▲◀ An etched and engraved champagne glass with a deep saucer-like bowl on a thin stem. This design was in vogue from about 1830 but is deeper than today's versions. The ample bowl probably held about 6floz of champagne.

PRICE GUIDE ❸

▲▲ A champagne flute with a long, engraved glass bowl. This design of glass was advertised from 1773 and was probably the first to be specifically used for champagne. The deep bowl and narrow neck prevent the bubbles escaping too quickly. Flutes are popular with today's champagne connoisseurs.

PRICE GUIDE ❸

PRICE GUIDE ▶

▼◀◀ *A simply designed water goblet, with cut indentations on the globular bowl. The waisted, hollow glass stem – blown from a section of glass rod – is topped and tailed with slim balusters of solid glass.*

PRICE GUIDE **3**

▼◀ *A highly decorated wine goblet, with a riot of the popular grapes and vineleaves engraved on the bowl, above a bulbous stem. The water jug behind it would also have been used for lemonade. It has an engraved top half and a diamond-cut lower half.*

PRICE GUIDE **4**

▲ *Sherry glasses come in a variety of shapes, from tall flutes downwards. The simple design of this particular glass has an ovoid bowl engraved with grapes and vineleaves.*

PRICE GUIDE **2**

▲ *The globular bowl of this port glass is engraved with a typical grape motif. There are finger-shaped indentations, or 'printies' at the base and the cut-glass stem is faceted.*

PRICE GUIDE **3**

▲ *A thistle glass for liqueurs. Delightfully made, the lower half of the waisted bowl is diamond-cut, while the upper half of the bowl has an engraved thistle design.*

PRICE GUIDE **3**

▼ *A cut-glass water goblet. There is an engraved heraldic image on the bowl above the band of diamond cutting. The stem has a bulbous lower portion and is also shaped by a method of facet cutting.*

PRICE GUIDE **4**

▲ *A plain champagne glass with a shallow saucer-shaped bowl. Above the broad foot, its thick, facetted stem is made of hollow glass. The saucer-shaped bowl, popular with the Victorians and indeed, well into this century, has now been replaced in fashion by the flute glass.*

The integral bowl and stem design was later used for sundae dishes.

PRICE GUIDE **5**

COLLECTOR'S TIPS

Etched Glass

THE MORE ELABORATE AND COMPLEX THE ETCHING, THE MORE VALUABLE THE PIECE. THE TUMBLER WITH THE ALL-OVER LEAFY PATTERN WILL FETCH MORE THAN ONE WITH A SIMPLE DESIGN.

Victorian table glass is such a large subject that the collector is often obliged to specialize, either in a particular style of glass or a theme, such as sherry glasses or decanters. Glass is widely available, although the uninitiated may have some trouble distinguishing a genuine Victorian piece from a later piece made in the Victorian style. The serious enthusiast would be well advised to visit museums and specialist dealers in order to become familiar with the wide range of shapes, colours and decorations prevalent in Victorian glassware.

MAKERS' MARKS

Victorian blown glass rarely had any identifiable markings. Cheaper pressed glass, however, was marked with a patent office 'lozenge' or registration mark between 1842 and 1883, and individual factories had their own particular impressed mark – a peacock's head for Sowerby and a demi-lion on a turret for Davidson.

Dates can be roughly estimated by the presence or absence of a pontil mark. The mark is simply a small lump of glass on the base, to which an iron rod or *pontil* was attached which the blower held while decorating the piece. Few glasses or decanters after 1850 had this mark – generally, there was just a small hollow where the mark was ground out – so its presence may indicate a forgery.

Damaged pieces are best avoided, as any small cracks weaken the glass considerably.

DEFECTS AND DAMAGE

It is possible to have small chips on the rims of glasses and decanters polished out by an expert although if the chip is too deep the damaged portion will have to be ground down considerably and the height of the piece altered. You can repair small chips on inexpensive items yourself using a diamond file available from specialist suppliers. Heavily cut glass is particularly susceptible to chips – always check a piece before you buy by running a finger round the rim and over the cut section. Decanter stoppers can also be ground to eliminate minor damage.

Defects in the glass itself or the design should mean a cheaper buy. Again, only experience and the handling of good pieces will enable you to spot a bad example.

The insides of decanters can be damaged by condensation, so check this carefully before any purchase. To avoid deterioration at home, always dry decanters carefully after washing. Several soft tissues or pieces of kitchen roll pushed around by a strong S-shaped piece of wire will clean the inside

The Shaft and Globe Decanter

THE VICTORIANS FAVOURED HEAVILY CUT DECANTERS AND THIS SHAFT AND GLOBE OR *ONION* STYLE WAS ONE OF THE MOST POPULAR DESIGNS. THIS FINE LEAD GLASS DECANTER WAS PROBABLY MANUFACTURED AROUND 1860 BY STEVENS AND WILLIAMS OF BRIERLEY HILL NEAR STOURBRIDGE. THE COMPANY STILL TRADES TODAY UNDER THE NAME OF BRIERLEY CRYSTAL.

THE ORNATELY-CUT DECORATION EXTENDS FROM THE STOPPER DOWN TO THE BASE, THE FINE CROSS-CUT DIAMOND PATTERN ON THE STOPPER REFLECTING THE PATTERN ON THE GLOBE. THE DIAMOND PATTERN IS OUTLINED WITH SAW-TOOTHED EDGED LOOPS, AS IS THE NECK OF THE STOPPER.

THE STOPPER ITSELF IS HOLLOW WITH AN OPEN BOTTOM, WHICH PROVED EXTREMELY USEFUL FOR SERVING A QUICK TIPPLE.

① HOLLOW CROSS-CUT DIAMOND GLASS STOPPER

② SCALE CUTTING ON THE NECK

③ CROSS-CUT DIAMOND PATTERNED GLOBE WITH LOOPED FRAME

④ OVERCUT STAR PATTERNED BASE

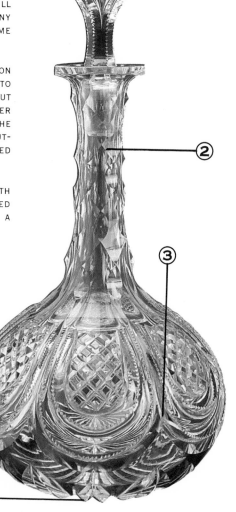

▲ *Two glass decanter stoppers. The one on the right has been badly chipped at the bottom but it is a fault that can be repaired. The stopper at left was chipped but has been ground down to a perfect finish.*

·*CLOSE UP*·

① A BLUE CASED CLARET JUG.

① A GLOBULAR CLARET JUG WITH AN ATTRACTIVE NATURAL DESIGN. THE MISSING STOPPER REDUCES ITS VALUE.

② THREE PATTERNS IN CUT GLASS: HOBNAILS DIVIDED BY DIAGONAL GROOVES WITH STARS.

③ THE GRAPE AND VINELEAF DESIGN OCCURS FREQUENTLY ON WINE GLASSES AND DECANTERS.

④ BEWARE OF MARRIAGES: THE STOPPER OF THIS JUG IS NOT ORIGINAL.

⑤ CUT-GLASS CLARET JUGS ARE OFTEN TOPPED WITH A SILVER SPOUT, LID AND HANDLE – CHECK FOR THE HALLMARK.

⑥ SILVER ADDED TO CLARET DECANTERS AND JUGS USUALLY HAS A DETAILED HALLMARK; SILVER-PLATE CARRIES THE MAKER'S MARK.

② THREE PATTERNS ON CUT GLASS.

③ ENGRAVED VINELEAF DESIGN.

⑤ HALLMARKS ON SILVER-TOPPED JUG.

④ ETCHED CLARET JUG.

⑥ MAKER'S MARK ON SILVER-PLATE.

successfully – if this proves difficult use a hairdryer on a low setting.

GOOD BUYS

Price varies according to quality, rarity, style and design, but most Victorian glass is quite reasonably priced. Complete sets fetch more than the sum total of their components as they are rare and highly sought-after. Common Victorian glasses such as those decorated with banded engraving are relatively cheap and easily found; it is possible to build up a set of similar patterns.

POINTS TO WATCH

■ Look over the glass carefully – cracks are often concealed by the deep faceting and brilliant cutting, and relief diamonds are prone to chipping.

■ Check the rims of wine glasses. If they are too flat and straight they may have been ground down in order to eliminate small chips.

■ The stopper should fit the decanter perfectly as each was ground individually to ensure an airtight seal. A loose stopper is not original.

▲ *Glasses were washed in rinsers between drinks.*

The Port Decanter

The ritual of 'passing the port' in its subtly decorated decanter
was a cherished part of any social gathering

Port has long been known as the Englishman's wine. Since the early 18th century, Englishmen have manufactured it in Portugal and shipped it home, and – more than any other nation – they have drunk it with vigour. 'It strengthens while it gladdens,' wrote George Saintsbury in his *Notes on a Wine Cellar.* 'There is something about it which must have been created in pre-established harmony with the best English character.'

In its heyday, port was far more than a glass or two after dinner. In *The Flowing Bowl,* a lively discourse on Victorian drinking customs, Edward Spencer recounts with awe how the men of his father's generation would routinely drink three or four bottles of port on a festive occasion. He tells of how 'after the retirement of the ladies to drink tea and discuss scandal by themselves, the dining room door would be locked by the host himself, who would pocket the key thereof. Many of the guests slept where they fell, whilst others would be fastened in the interior of their chariots at a later hour.' Even allowing for a certain imaginative embroidery in this description, the figures tell much the same story: in 1887, when lighter wines were growing in popularity, 22 per cent of all wine consumed in Great Britain was still port, French wines accounting for 40 per cent and Spanish for 20 per cent.

Considering that the price of port made it largely a

◀ *With the growing popularity of port from the 18th century on, it became necessary to improve both storage and serving methods. Although the decanter had originally been used only for wine, it became more and more popular for port, since the airtight stopper helped to preserve this traditional after-dinner drink.*

wine for the wealthy, it can be assumed that for many an old-fashioned Victorian gentleman, port was the *vin de table* as well as the preferred beverage in the smoking and billiard rooms. When cigars were alight and the decanter of '47 was passed around the table – always from right to left, as the foreigner soon learned – it was port that filled the glasses. And it was port that caused the billiard balls to swim on an ocean of green baize as an elderly gentleman steadied himself for one final shot before the footman helped him up to bed.

The port decanter, which played such a central part in this clockwise after-dinner ritual, was essentially the same as that used for sherry, Madeira or other popular fortified wines. It has its origins in the bulbous, long necked decanter bottle used in the 17th century for serving wine from the cask at the table. Since this method also ensured that bottled wine could be served free of sediment, the decanter, as it was known by the early 18th century, rapidly became a permanent piece of tableware.

EARLY DESIGNS

Georgian designers were quick to develop many of the basic shapes that have persisted into this century. These included bottle-shaped and bell-shaped decanters, club-shaped decanters with straight, sloping sides and a shoulder, the wide-based ship's decanter and square-sectioned whisky decanters. Standard sizes included the pint, the quart and the double quart, or magnum. Decanters used for fortified wines or spirits were provided with tightly fitting ground-glass stoppers to keep out the air. Towards the end of the century, most circular decanters were made with two or three raised rings around the neck, to ensure a good grip for a possibly unsteady hand.

Some decanters were engraved with a description of their contents. Port, sherry, and Madeira are three of the most frequently encountered. Most, however, were unnamed. Their contents were generally identified by engraved silver labels hung around their necks.

AN EXPLOSION OF GLASSWARE

Early Victorian designers and manufacturers approached the decanter with the same naive exuberance that they brought to all useful or decorative objects. Their enthusiasm for glassware is partly explained by the repeal, in 1845, of the stringent excise duties which had taxed glass objects by their weight for the previous 100 years. Prior to this date, glass manufacturers thought twice before adding a foot or a handle to a decanter, or a few more inches to its height; suddenly all such restrictions were lifted. The result was a burgeoning of all glass manufacture and new life for the heavy, ornate decanter.

To satisfy the public's love of novelty, Victorians borrowed nearly every decanter design of the previous century, and added a few of their own. Although there was no one 'typical' Victorian decanter, fashions gradually changed from the cylindrical Georgian style to a bulbous-bodied, narrow-necked design. This evolved into an extremely popular late Victorian decanter shape – an imitation of ancient Greek pottery with a slender, unringed neck above an egg-shaped body resting on a base or foot. Stoppers were another important part of decanter design; typical shapes included mushrooms, cartwheels, balls and pinnacles.

CUT GLASS

Regency decanters were often ornately cut, and the early Victorians followed this fashion, but the vogue for cut-glass decoration declined somewhat with the introduction, in the 1830s, of press-moulded glass from America, which looked like cut glass to all but the expert – and cost a fraction of the price to produce. On top of this, the eminent critic John

▲ *A post-prandial glass of port was commonplace at the social gatherings of upper-class gentlemen, and was rarely consumed in the presence of ladies.*

Decanter Styles

A CRYSTAL DECANTER DATING FROM 1890 WITH A HALLMARKED SILVER NECK.

A CRYSTAL DECANTER C. 1840 WITH ENGRAVED GRAPE MOTIFS.

THIS CRYSTAL DECANTER DATES FROM 1870 AND IS OF THE SHAFT AND GLOBE DESIGN.

Ruskin had dismissed all cut glass as 'barbarous', a decree which encouraged progressive members of the public to favour plainer glassware.

For those Victorians who did not admire plain surfaces, there were a variety of decorative finishes to choose from. A technique known as overlay, or flashing, in which two or more colours of glass were superimposed and then decoratively cut, was popular Decanters were also engraved with flowers, ferns, fruit, vines and sporting or classical scenes. Etching with acid was a cheaper technique, which gave much the same effect as engraving. This involved etching a pattern in a protective overlay, then applying acid which ate into the surface of the glass.

Victorians loved coloured glass. The rich blues and greens of the Bristol factories were particularly popular, while pinkish-red 'cranberry' glass was a passion for some collectors. On the whole, delicate tints such as apple green, amber, amethyst and straw opal were more popular than dark colours. Sometimes colours were simply applied as decorative strips across the surface of a plain glass decanter. However, because wine itself is such an attractive colour, and because the English were world-famous for the brilliance of their plain leaded glass, most decanters remained uncoloured.

DECANTER SETS

Decanters frequently came in sets – a pint, a quart and a claret decanter comprising a typical combination. The young couple setting up on their own, however, might look for a set with matching glasses as well. Perhaps they would turn to the Harrods catalogue, which in 1895 was selling 87-piece suites, including a set of 12 glasses each for sherry, port, claret and champagne. A port glass was typically somewhat smaller than a claret glass, but the Victo-

rians were surprisingly unfussy about how they took their favourite drink. Mrs Beeton, in her classic *Household Management*, reckoned that while a port glass could be too small, it could not be too big, and recounted approvingly of an old acquaintance, 'a connoisseur of port', who put before his guests glasses 'holding nearly a pint'.

The tantalus, a stand containing a set of cut-glass

▲ *For a special occasion such as a wedding reception, the decanter set which included champagne glasses and a matching selection of sherry, port and claret glasses to go with the various courses, was ideal.*

DECANTERS AND GLASSES

Decanters and glasses vary greatly in price depending on the method and intricacy of decoration, with 18th-century engraved decanters costing up to £2,000 and plain late 19th-century ones costing as little as £10. Glasses can also be found from £10 to £250.

▲ *These four matching port glasses were made in 1830 by Voneche of Belgium and are elaborately cut with unusual geometric patterns.*

PRICE GUIDE **5**

◀ *This simply-designed tantalus, dating from the early 1900s, is made in mahogany and silver and contains three hobnail cut-crystal decanters with many-faceted ball stoppers. The wooden base has mounts fashioned in electroplated silver, matching the handle.*

PRICE GUIDE ❼

decanters, was popular with Victorian householders who wished to preserve their liquor for themselves rather than their servants. It was named after Tantalus, the tortured Greek of mythology, who stood, parched, up to his neck in water unable to take a drink. This ingenious device displayed the decanters in a locked rack, teasing the thirsty butler with a sight, but never a sip, of the vintage port.

A more generous device for holding decanter sets was the silver decanter trolley, a tiny four-wheeled vehicle, which was pushed around the table top (always from right to left), presumably to save one's guests from straining their arms and shoulders. The baize-bottomed wine coaster, or bottle slide, was used for the same purpose.

By the end of the Victorian era, the great age of port had passed. Whisky, gin-and-bitters and the table wines of France had 'wiped out', as Edward Spencer lamented in 1899, 'the age when man drank, talked and thought port'.

▼ *This magnum-sized decanter actually holds up to half a gallon of port. It was produced by Voneche of Belgium in 1810 and has rather less engraving than the typically elaborate Regency designs of the previous century. The use of colourless glass reflects its growing popularity in the 19th century.*

PRICE GUIDE ❼

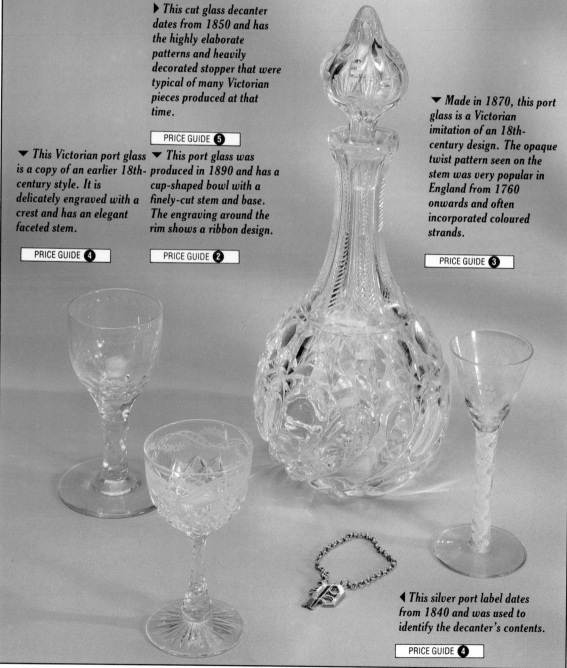

▶ *This cut glass decanter dates from 1850 and has the highly elaborate patterns and heavily decorated stopper that were typical of many Victorian pieces produced at that time.*

PRICE GUIDE ❺

▼ *This Victorian port glass is a copy of an earlier 18th-century style. It is delicately engraved with a crest and has an elegant faceted stem.*

PRICE GUIDE ❹

▼ *This port glass was produced in 1890 and has a cup-shaped bowl with a finely-cut stem and base. The engraving around the rim shows a ribbon design.*

PRICE GUIDE ❷

▼ *Made in 1870, this port glass is a Victorian imitation of an 18th-century design. The opaque twist pattern seen on the stem was very popular in England from 1760 onwards and often incorporated coloured strands.*

PRICE GUIDE ❸

◀ *This silver port label dates from 1840 and was used to identify the decanter's contents.*

PRICE GUIDE ❹

Cruets

Essential for the Edwardian dining table, elegant silver and
cut-glass cruets for oil, vinegar and sauce are now very popular
with collectors

No Victorian or Edwardian dining room with any pretension to style would have been without a cruet set to grace the table. Most consisted of a silver-footed stand, with a carrying handle, usually containing four bottles – for salt, pepper, vinegar and mustard.

Nowadays, there is a tendency to think of 'cruet' as the name for salt and pepper sets. In fact, it derives from a Dutch word meaning 'crock' and signifies a small earthenware bottle, shaped rather like a decanter, which was used to hold olive oil or vinegar for salad dressing.

FRENCH ORIGINS

As salad dressing was a French habit, it is likely that cruets originated in France and first made their way to Britain in the late 17th century. At that time, they were found only in the most wealthy and fashionable houses.

Ordinary households would have had a salt cellar on the table – a shallow dish with a matching spoon – and perhaps a pepper pot made of pewter, glass or porcelain. Many surviving examples of 17th-century cruets are made of flint glass and have a distinctive mallet shape. Those produced in the 18th century were generally taller with bulbous bodies, although more slender shapes became popular towards the end of the century.

The earliest cruet sets usually consisted of two bottles in a carrying frame and were more likely to be used for water and wine at Communion than salad dressing on the dining table. Those designed for household use frequently held five or more containers: three with perforated tops (called casters), used for dry condiments like salt, pepper and sugar; and at least two bottles for oil and vinegar, or spicier condiments, such as mustard or hot pepper sauce. These larger five-bottle sets are usually known as 'Warwick cruets' after their use at Warwick Castle as early as 1715.

'Soy frames', also known as 'sauce bottle stands', became quite common in the mid-18th century. These held a variety of condiments, including oil, vinegar, soy sauce, ketchup, chutney, mustard, lemon and, increasingly, shop-bought sauces, all usually identified by a small silver ticket around the neck of the bottle.

BREAKFAST CRUETS

By the early 19th century cruets had become smaller, although frames often contained as many as ten bottles. These smaller sets were known as 'breakfast cruets'. Although sets consisting of only salt, pepper and mustard pot were produced *en suite* from the 18th century onwards, this style did not become the norm until the late 19th century. By Edwardian

times, sets containing more than three or four bottles would have been considered excessive.

The cruet sets first introduced to England consisted of silver stands with silver-mounted glass bottles – probably made by Huguenot silversmiths. The fashion for silver continued throughout the 18th century, when designs drew on classical influences and became more fanciful. The silver was usually richly engraved with elaborately decorated caster tops. After 1770 many more cruets were made from fused plate and rolled silver. A particularly popular 18th-century Adam-style cruet set comprised a boat-shaped stand decorated with rams' heads and swags, and contained two ewer-shaped bottles.

A VARIETY OF MATERIALS

With the advent of mass production came the technique of pressing glass into a mould rather than blowing it. While this proved to be quick and cheap, pressed glass has none of the brilliance associated

▼ *A collection of cruets with two to five bottles, all made in silver and glass. Earlier cruets were made in flint glass, which was lavishly cut in faceted patterns to reflect the light; later sets were plainer.*

▲ Later additions to the table were salt and pepper shakers, and egg cruets and boilers. Many of these are made in electro-plated nickel silver or Sheffield plate, although some were also made in porcelain. The egg boiler, with its egg cups and spoons, meant that eggs could be freshly cooked at the table and then served in the accompanying cups.

with genuine cut glass, so although it is still highly collectable, it remains the 'poor relation' as far as glassware is concerned.

The use of porcelain and pottery for cruet sets became more commonplace towards the end of the 19th century, and was quite widespread by Edwardian times. In fact, china dinner services were not considered complete without a matching cruet set, and all major pottery manufacturers produced them in large numbers.

Porcelain and pottery cruets usually had some form of painted decoration, often flowers or rural scenes. They were often inscribed with the name of the contents, or embellished with inscriptions such as 'Souvenir of Southend'. Many also came in novelty shapes, frequently with the aim of disguising their functional purpose. Carlton, for example, manufactured cruets in the shape of flowers and tomatoes, while Grimwades produced some in the popular cottage ware style.

SOUVENIR CRUETS

More frequently, however, they were mass-produced for the gift market, being popular holiday souvenirs. Many were produced in Leeds creamware and Lowestoft ware, and came in all shapes and sizes: figures in national costume, windmills (complete with rotating sails), and all manner of wild animals were some of the innovations on the market. Other manufacturers produced them in glass, porcelain, various metals, and early plastics, such as Bakelite.

With any collection of cruets, it is most important that the set should be complete and undamaged. The stand adds considerably to the value, so make sure it is intact and that all the bottles fit properly and are all the same height.

Glass cruets should be unchipped and have their original, matching stoppers. Cut glass is the most desirable, and the quality of the cutting and faceting is really more important than the silver mounts or stands. Look for clean cutting and brilliance. Pressed or moulded glass is more commonplace, but is much duller. Where glass cruets have silver mounts, check the hallmarks to make sure you have matching pieces.

Genuine silver pieces often have full sets of hallmarks on the stand, handle and mounts. The feet of the stand should be neither bent, cracked nor missing. Many popular patterns were reproduced in silver plate, so do ensure that no item within a silver set has been replaced with a replica in silver-plate.

▲ *A rather unusually shaped cruet in electroplated nickel silver and glass, taking its inspiration from the thistle, a symbol that was very popular as a decorative motif in late Victorian times.*

DECORATIVE FEATURES

Glass cruets were cut into intricate designs so that they could complement the rest of a table setting. The quality of the faceting is of particular importance to collectors in assessing the value of a piece. From about 1730 onwards, patterns were also cut by the abrasive action of a revolving wheel used with sand-based powders, a technique which was known as wheel-engraving.

Victorian and Edwardian cruets, particularly those with silver plating, frequently incorporated ornate embossing or etching on the stand with beaded edging. The feet are usually a good indication of the period from which a cruet comes: early stands have ball and claw or hoof feet, while later ones are generally plain.

·PRICE GUIDE· ⟩ CRUET SETS

Cruet prices tend to be high in relation to their size. Early cruets are relatively difficult to come by, hence their high prices. A simple three-bottle set in a boat-shaped stand, made in 1781, is worth £1200, while a more elaborate five-bottle set from the same period reaches £2500. Victorian silver-plate is much more accessible, however, and *although prices have recently soared, it is still possible to find sets for as little as £50-£60. Finely cut glass cruets cost from £20-£70, while pressed glass examples range from £10-£20. Pottery cruets dating from the turn of the 20th century can often be picked up for a few pounds. Egg boilers and cruets cost from £80-£100.*

Deco Table Glass

Drinking was a fashionable activity between the wars, and top
designers produced glasses, decanters and cocktail shakers in
typical Art Deco styles and materials

Though the 1920s and 1930s were
hard times for some, for others they
seemed one continuous party that
moved from country house weekends to
London balls and night clubs. Alcohol –
especially champagne and cocktails – fuelled
the rounds of the smart set, and few things
encapsulate the brittle gaiety of their lives
better than the decorated glasses, decanters
and other drinking accessories of the time.

TRADITION AND INNOVATION

A tradition of conservatism characterized
the British glass industry in the first decades
of this century, with Victorian designs
dominating well after World War I.
Glasses and decanters were typically of
heavy cut glass, with every square inch
smothered in rich, over-elaborate designs.

The impetus for change came both from
within, from a jazz-age public seeking ever
more modern designs, and from the increasing outside influence of continental glass-

Cocktail Shaker

A VERY UNUSUAL 1930S' COCKTAIL
SHAKER, WITH A BLUE GLASS BASE AND
HAND-PAINTED WOODCOCK DESIGN.

▼ *In smart houses and top hotels the cocktail bar was a wonderland of exotic bottles, silver shakers and chic glasses. The barmen of the time used exciting combinations to devise new cocktails, serving them with panache.*

▶ *Cocktails and a book of cocktail recipes. The Savoy Cocktail Book was the 'bible' of many barmen in the 1930s and silver cocktail shakers often incorporated lists of ingredients.*

makers. The French makers who were the stars of the 1925 Exhibition of Decorative Arts in Paris revived old techniques and perfected new ones, creating a range of colourful new styles both for mass-produced items and limited edition and one-off pieces of art glass. Almost as influential was a 1931 London exhibition of Swedish glass by firms such as Kosta Glasbruk AB and Orrefors, displaying simple, elegant forms and restrained, unfussy engraved decoration. The two influences, colourful experimentation and sculptural form, were incorporated into the manufacture of British drinking glass, alongside the stock-in-trade Victorian and Regency reproductions.

BRITISH GLASS

Few British firms produced art glass on the French model – Moncrieff in Scotland with their Monart pieces and Gray-Stan in London were the exceptions – but many of the mass-production companies employed top-line designers. Clyne Farquharson at John Walsh Walsh and the New Zealander Keith Murray at Stevens & Williams were the most feted; both produced stylish pieces influenced by Swedish designs.

Stuart and Sons commissioned outside designers and artists such as Paul Nash, Graham Sutherland and Laura Knight to design glassware for a British Art in Industry exhibition at the Royal Academy. Some of their designs were for unornamented coloured glass, while others were decorated with cuts, swirls and cross-hatching. Laura Knight used engraved, stylized human figures such as clowns and skaters and yellow, black and red enamels. Though none of the designs went into full production, they were a great influence on late-1930s drinking glasses.

TECHNICAL INNOVATIONS

The French developed new techniques for incorporating metallic oxides – cobalt for blue, uranium for yellow, iron for green, and so on – to produce hard, shiny glass that made thinner but more durable drinking glasses.

The late 19th-century technique of pâte de verre, where ground glass and metallic oxides were made into a paste that could be moulded and fired like pottery, was perfected in the 1920s in France and was sometimes used to make decanters, trays and glasses. These were necessarily expensive as each was a one-off creation, and French pâte de verre work found its way into only the smartest homes.

Much commoner, but no less stylish, were pieces decorated with metallic enamels; wedges or bands of black, pioneered by the Steuben factory in the USA and Baccarat in France, were typically Deco.

Coloured enamels were combined with transfer prints in widely available decanter and glass sets. In Britain these usually took the form of hunting scenes, flowers, butterflies, even spiders, rather than the more modern Deco patterns, which were usually coloured stripes and spots or jazzy renditions of dancers, devils or lucky charms.

Engraving with a copper wheel was an ancient method of decorating glass, but was enormously time-consuming. It resisted mechanization and was therefore expensive. Costs were reduced in the 1920s and 1930s with the development of intaglio, a combination of cutting and engraving, where the fine detail only was produced with the wheel; the cutting gave depth to the decoration, the engraving lent lightness.

The work of the great modern glassmakers was sold in Britain in just a few stores such as Fortnum and Mason's and Heal's in London and Marshall and Snelgrove in Leicester, but the mass-produced wares influenced by, or in some cases plainly imitating, them were available at every local department store. They brought Art Deco style, with just a touch of the glamour attached to the smart set, to millions of British homes.

Cocktail Glass

The inter-war years were the heyday of the cock-tail, which reached Britain from America in 1919, just as Prohibition was introduced. Almost every cocktail ever invented, from the White Lady to the vividly-coloured Pousse Cafés (layers of rainbow-coloured cordial liqueurs carefully poured to prevent them mixing), first appeared in the 1920s and 1930s and went in and out of fashion with bewildering speed. The combination of novelty and the ritual of preparing and drinking cocktails helped make them the perfect drink for the times.

Along with the smart new drinks came a demand for smart new glasses. The glasses developed to meet this demand had a plain stem ending in a ball, from the top of which flared out a broad, shallow, conical bowl. They were typically of clear glass decorated with bands of enamelled colour; red and black were the most common. Accompanying the glasses were shakers of glass and chrome, some functionally simple, others with a great deal of novelty value. Long swizzle sticks for stirring cocktails were usually made of metal, though some made of glass in various colours survive.

Ice buckets — for cubed, crushed or shaved ice — were generally lined with clear glass, while the drinks were served on a tray of reflective coloured glass with a chrome or silver trim or finish.

▶ *Hanging from a chase plate stand, these 1930s glass swizzle sticks have red Bakelite knobs.*

PRICE GUIDE ❸

▶ *An elegant English-made cocktail shaker. The stopper, in the shape of a cockerel's head, sits inside a glass strainer which is separate from the etched body.*

PRICE GUIDE ❺

▼ *A set of six unusual cocktail glasses. Made of glass, they are silvered inside and out, with black decoration.*

PRICE GUIDE ❺

◀ *A 1930s chrome and cut crystal cocktail shaker. Paddles inside stir the ingredients together.*

PRICE GUIDE **3**

◀ *A frosted glass decanter and matching glasses. The glasses are silver rimmed and the decanter is decorated with irregular spots.*

PRICE GUIDE **5**

▲ *Classically shaped 1930s cocktail glasses with black glass stems and bases. They are labelled for Pink Lady cocktails.*

PRICE GUIDE **3**

▲ *A cocktail set in yellow glass, made by James Powell and Sons Ltd at Whitefriars Glass Works.*

PRICE GUIDE **5**

PRICE GUIDE

Glass Sets

Sets of glasses and tumblers with matching jugs or decanters were made in great numbers in the 1930s and were considered an ideal gift item. Many have survived as they were put into display cases rather than used.

Generally sets were of six glasses with other pieces as appropriate. Whisky sets, for instance, had six shot glasses with a decanter and a water jug, cocktail sets had a shaker, while lemonade sets, lager sets and water sets had tall, usually straight-sided jugs and half-pint tumblers.

Some manufacturers made sets in coloured glass – Whitefriars for example made many in emerald green – but most were produced in decorated clear glass. Modernism was expressed in simple incised line decoration, as by the Stevens & Williams; colour was introduced by a mix of transfer printing and enamelling.

Sometimes the sets matched in both pattern and colour, but Harlequin sets, with each glass having the same pattern but a different colour, were popular not only with the public but also with the manufacturers, who no longer had to produce batches of glasses of exactly the same shades.

Wine sets tended to follow the conservative designs of Victorian sets, in coloured or cut glass, or reproduction Regency styles, but whisky, liqueur and cocktail sets attracted top Deco designers. The Baccarat factory for example made chunky liqueur glasses accompanied by angular decanters strikingly decorated with black enamels, designed by Georges Chevalier or André Ballet. The stoppers, as with many Deco decanters, were large and similarly enamelled.

French designers used every available new technique in making drink sets. Some of the most striking types were the cubist-inspired sets in pâte de verre made complete with trays in the same material.

▼ *A wine decanter set decorated with areas of pink etching and delicate etched lines. The glasses have elegant slim stems and the decanter has a ground glass stopper.*

PRICE GUIDE 4

▶ *A stylish Deco liqueur set. Designed three-dimensionally, the heart-shaped decanter and glasses are decorated with abstract patterns.*

PRICE GUIDE 7

▶ *A lemonade or water jug and matching conical glasses in frosted glass, with red and white spots and concentric red rings.*

PRICE GUIDE 4

▲ A tall, straight-sided lemonade
or water set in tinted glass,
enlivened by bands of gold in
varying widths.

PRICE GUIDE ④

▲ Part of a classic sherry set with
engraved pattern. Each piece is
signed by the designer, Clyne
Farquharson, of John Walsh Walsh.

PRICE GUIDE ⑧

▲ A colourful, hard-wearing Deco
lemonade or water set in plain
glass, with bands of colour and a
peppermint green base and rim.

PRICE GUIDE ④

PRICE GUIDE

COLLECTOR'S TIPS

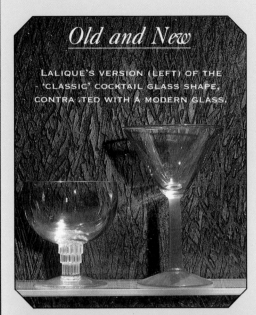

Old and New

LALIQUE'S VERSION (LEFT) OF THE 'CLASSIC' COCKTAIL GLASS SHAPE, CONTRASTED WITH A MODERN GLASS.

Most writers on the Art Deco period tend to focus on art glass by major designers, or on glass used in architecture and interior design. Such items, though, are in short supply, and often difficult to display, so tableware, for a long time the Cinderella glassware of the period, is now becoming highly collectable.

For better or worse, this means that lemonade, liqueur or cocktail sets which could not be given away ten years ago are now making hundreds of pounds, even though their provenance is rarely known. Very few glass manufacturers marked their work.

BUYING DECO TABLE GLASS

However, the high prices are mostly confined to a few specialist, expert London dealers. The craze for Art Deco glass is recent enough for the news to have failed to percolate down to small traders at boot sales and flea markets, and there are bargains still to be had for those who study the field carefully.

The biggest problem is in deciding whether a piece is genuine Art Deco, postwar revival or even a fake; sometimes, even the experts cannot tell the difference. Style is the all-important guide, so you cannot look at too many pieces in shops, museums and catalogues before taking the plunge and buying some for yourself.

Certain types are too expensive and too difficult to fake and some are not yet expensive enough to make faking a piece worth the trouble. Some of the less extravagant mirror and gilt glass sets, for instance, or the plain mass-produced cocktail glasses, are reliable collectors' items, though there is

Cocktail Shaker & Glasses

TODAY'S TYPICAL COCKTAIL GLASS IS AN INVERTED CONE ON A SLIM, CYLINDRICAL STEM RISING FROM A CIRCULAR BASE. BUT WHEN COCKTAILS WERE INTRODUCED IN THE 1920S THE GLASSES DESIGNED FOR THEM CAME IN A WIDE VARIETY OF SHAPES. THE DRINKS WERE NEW AND NEW GLASSES EVOLVED TO ACCOMMODATE THEM. AT FIRST THEY WERE BASED ON EXISTING LIQUEUR GLASSES AND TUMBLERS, DECORATED WITH CONTEMPORARY DESIGNS. THE SET SHOWN HERE IS IN THAT VEIN. IN SHAPE THE GLASSES RESEMBLE WHISKY TUMBLERS BUT THEIR DECORATION IS QUINTESSENTIALLY DECO. THE COCKTAIL SHAKER ITSELF WAS, OF COURSE, A NEW INVENTION, DESIGNED TO SHAKE OR STIR THE MIXTURE OF DRINKS AND SIEVE OUT FRUIT OR ICE WHEN POURING.

① A FROSTED DIAMOND PATTERN ETCHED INTO THE GLASS

② BLACK LINES, INTERSPERSED WITH SILVER SQUARES, SEPARATE THE FROSTED DIAMONDS

③ THE CHROME-PLATED POURER HAS A BUILT-IN STRAINER, A COMMON FEATURE OF COCKTAIL SHAKERS

④ THE SHAKER AND GLASSES HAVE RELATIVELY HEAVY GLASS BOTTOMS, LIKE WHISKY TUMBLERS

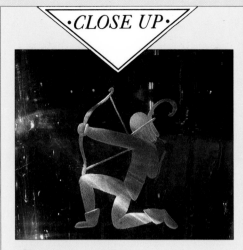

① ENGRAVED DESIGN

③ ETCHED DESIGN

④ MOULDED GLASS

② TIERED STEM

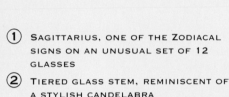

① SAGITTARIUS, ONE OF THE ZODIACAL
   SIGNS ON AN UNUSUAL SET OF 12
   GLASSES

② TIERED GLASS STEM, REMINISCENT OF
   A STYLISH CANDELABRA

③ AN ELEGANT FROSTED EFFECT
   PRODUCED BY ETCHING

④ A MOULDED GLASS COCKEREL'S HEAD
   FORMS THE HEAD OF A STOPPER

⑤ SILVERED AND BLACK PAINTED SPOTS
   IN AN EYE-CATCHING DESIGN.

⑤ DECO SPOTS

always the possibility that they were made in the USA during – or just after – World War II.

Contemporary catalogues from the top department stores such as Heal's, Liberty's, Harrods or the Army and Navy Stores, as well as advertisements from the style magazines of the period such as *Design*, are an excellent guide to what was fashionable; they can be bought from dealers in ephemera or consulted in some of the big city reference libraries. Equally, reputable dealers are eager to help and will guide you through their stock. Attending auctions to see what is being sold as 1920s and 1930s glassware will help build up a feel for the period.

CARE AND DISPLAY
Glassware has an inbuilt rarity factor owing to its fragility: small, much-used and easily-broken items like drinking glasses will therefore always be sought-after. A bunch of odd drinking glasses displayed randomly in a glass case, however, is not particularly interesting to look at, so it pays to specialize rather than snap up any glass that is offered. Complete sets of glasses with decanters or jugs are getting harder to find, but look very well in a period, glass-lined display cabinet or, best of all, a genuine 1920s or 1930s cocktail cabinet.

Glassware is easy to maintain. Keep it clean by washing in plain soap and water – *never* in a dishwasher – and when polishing it, add a little jeweller's rouge to the cloth to give it extra sparkle. Use chamois leather or a modern substitute for polishing.

POINTS TO WATCH
■ Many decanters have lost their stoppers in the course of time; make sure the stopper matches the decanter in age and style.
■ Check glassware carefully for minute chips and cracks.
■ Watch out for highly collectable items not normally made of glass, such as cocktail shakers and swizzle sticks.

▲ *An American novelty decanter in red glass.*

Regency Oil Lamps

Improved types of oil lamps revolutionized lighting in the
Regency period, dispelling gloom and making living rooms
more cheerful and congenial places

Men and women have used lamps of one kind or another since very early times. Stone, pottery, bronze, iron, brass and many other metals have been fashioned to make them, and, where necessary, horn and glass have provided the required window materials. The simplest form of lamp – a wick floating in an open saucer filled with oil – has always found users, but more sophisticated models were available even in ancient times. Large numbers of Roman lamps have survived, the most characteristic type having a flattened, circular body, with a stoppered hole in the top through which the oil could be fed in, a spout for the wick, and in some cases a conveniently large round handle.

EARLY OIL LAMPS

Although many elaborate and beautiful lamps, often with multiple spouts, were made through the ages, until the 18th century there were only minor advances in lamp technology. In fact, oil lamps were by no means the most favoured form of lighting, since they had serious disadvantages by comparison with candles and rushlights. Their smell was unpleasant – especially if they had been fed with fish oil – and they could be damagingly smoky; in 1770 the Duke of Bedford's housekeeper inspected his bed and found it 'so very black with burning of oil in the room that she thinks it proper to have it cleaned'. However, it was at least possible to keep the ceiling relatively free from sooty deposits by placing smoke bells – large glass globes – over the table lamps in rooms throughout the house.

Filling and cleaning oil lamps and trimming their wicks made them tiresome to maintain. But their greatest disadvantage was that they were more expensive than good quality beeswax candles without giving much more light. On grand occasions hosts and hostesses displayed their wealth and status by lighting rooms with hundreds of candles blazing in splendid glass chandeliers hanging from the ceiling, or placed in candelabra on the mantelpiece or table.

This kind of scene, evoked in so many 18th-century letters and memoirs, was actually untypical of everyday life. The constant, heavy cost of lighting – whether done by wax or oil – strained the finances of even the rich, and stringent economies were practised in the highest places. In 1722 the Duchess of Northumberland reported that Queen Charlotte's dressing room, 'being very large and hung with crimson damask', was very dark, 'there being only 4 candles on the toilet' [dressing table], so that the King himself had to take one of the candles with him in order to show his visitor some-

▶ *The improvement in oil lamps in the late Georgian and Regency eras added brilliance and ease to social gatherings. This fashionable soirée is illuminated by a hanging brass lamp with four burners, and a standing lamp with an unusual shade sheds light upon the company around the table.*

◀ *On quiet evenings at home, the Regency family would gather round the table to read, sew or play cards. The oil lamp provided just enough light for these pastimes and helped to create a cosy atmosphere. Today, Regency lamps can add an authentic touch to a room decorated in period style.*

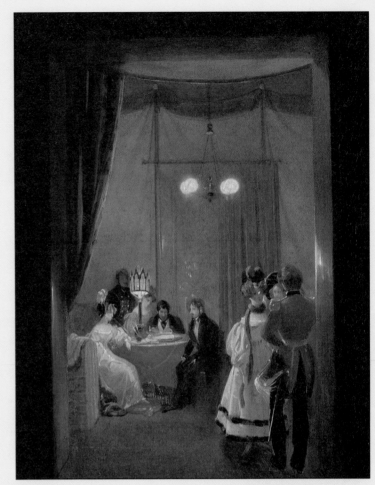

thing in another part of the room. The royal couple were admittedly notorious for their 'middle class' way of life, but it can hardly be doubted that when only the family were present, most Georgian parlours and drawing rooms were places that would strike us as gloomy and inconveniently under-lit – a fact that was bound to have an important influence on social behaviour.

18TH-CENTURY IMPROVEMENTS

All this changed due to a number of improvements that were made to oil lamps during the 18th century; among other things, the plaited cotton wick was introduced, and a central burner and glass case came to be used in place of the traditional spout on the edge of the lamp. But the major breakthrough came in the late Georgian period, in 1783, when the Swiss scientist Ami Argand invented a new kind of burner with a circular wick encased between two tubes; soon a glass funnel was added to protect the flame, and the result was a far more brilliant light than that given by any candle.

BRITISH ARGAND LAMPS

The famous inventor James Watt and his partner Matthew Boulton manufactured Argand lamps at their Soho Plate Company in Birmingham from 1784 onwards, but since their patent was overthrown, other manufacturers soon followed suit.

Further improvements were incorporated in the Carcel lamp (invented in 1800) and the Moderator lamp (which followed in 1835), making it possible to light rooms more brightly than before, at a fraction of the cost. Apart from making evening interiors much more cheerful, this facilitated important changes in British customs and habits. Families no longer needed to huddle close to the fire for light as well as heat, and one or more tables, each bearing a lamp, could be brought out into the middle of the room. Gathered around the tables, people could sit and talk, read and sew, an arrangement that allowed for both domestic togetherness and the amorous tête-à-tête. Better lighting was therefore an important factor in the increased domesticity, intimacy and informality characteristic of Regency life.

COAL GAS LAMPS

The Regency also gave birth to an even more revolutionary form of lighting, using coal gas. This was developed from 1792 by the engineer Richard Murdoch and taken up by his employers Boulton and Watt. By 1815 many London streets were gas-lit, and by the mid-19th century gas lighting had become common in the home. But oil lamps of the type pioneered in the Regency period survived for a surprisingly long time, finally succumbing late in the 19th century to competition from gas, electricity and the paraffin (petroleum-based) lamp.

Table and Wall Lamps

The brilliance of the Argand lamp, which could function both as a table- and as a wall-lamp, was based on two important innovations. Enclosing the hollow wick between two tubes brought it into contact with a double current of air, resulting in improved combustion and increased output. And placing a glass funnel or chimney above the burner increased the draught and further intensified the brightness of the flame, especially after one of Argand's competitors discovered the benefits of narrowing the glass towards the top.

Other technical details were significant in determining the effectiveness and also the distinctive shapes of Regency oil lamps. They ran on colza oil, which was made from a kind of kale called rape-seed. Thick and heavy, colza would not seep up the wick, so the reservoir feeding oil to the burner had to be operated by gravity, and was therefore placed above and to one side of it.

The problem was that this high reservoir threw an irritatingly large shadow. One solution was to surround the burner with a thin, ring-shaped reservoir, as in the Astral lamp introduced in about 1819. The Carcel lamp featured a clockwork pump that forced oil up from below, while the sturdier Moderator achieved the same effect with a spiral spring. Ultimately, in the early Victorian period, paraffin – which works by capillary action – did away with the problem of feeding the oil to the wick.

▶ *A brass student's lamp from the early 19th century, with a finger ring at the top of the stand to enable the user to carry it from room to room. The burner can be moved up and down the support.*

PRICE GUIDE ❹

◀ *An attractive Regency bronze table lamp in the neoclassical style. Although it has been adapted to electricity, it was originally fuelled by the colza oil contained in the urn-shaped reservoir.*

PRICE GUIDE ❼

PRICE GUIDE

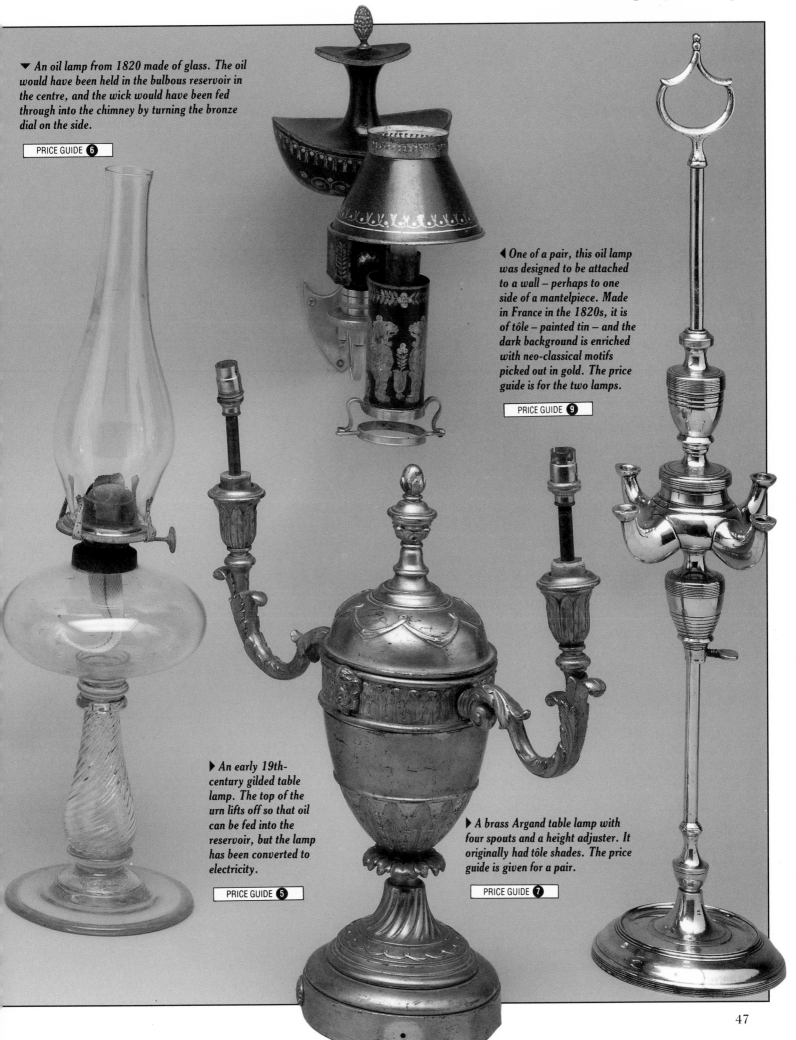

▼ *An oil lamp from 1820 made of glass. The oil would have been held in the bulbous reservoir in the centre, and the wick would have been fed through into the chimney by turning the bronze dial on the side.*

PRICE GUIDE **6**

◀ *One of a pair, this oil lamp was designed to be attached to a wall – perhaps to one side of a mantelpiece. Made in France in the 1820s, it is of tôle – painted tin – and the dark background is enriched with neo-classical motifs picked out in gold. The price guide is for the two lamps.*

PRICE GUIDE **9**

▶ *An early 19th-century gilded table lamp. The top of the urn lifts off so that oil can be fed into the reservoir, but the lamp has been converted to electricity.*

PRICE GUIDE **5**

▶ *A brass Argand table lamp with four spouts and a height adjuster. It originally had tôle shades. The price guide is given for a pair.*

PRICE GUIDE **7**

▲ Round green glass hanging lamp with a bronze collar, finial and chain. The wick would have floated in the oil.

PRICE GUIDE **5**

▲ Clear glass oil lamp with plain bronze fittings. Lack of detail or a manufacturer's mark make it difficult to date precisely, although it was probably made in the mid-19th century.

PRICE GUIDE **6**

▲▶ An unusual and elegant thistle-shaped glass lamp with a holder in the bottom showing that it has been adapted for use with candle rather than oil.

PRICE GUIDE **7**

Hanging Lamps

Lamps of many different types, materials and styles were made during the Georgian and Regency periods. In 1786 Sophie von La Roche, a German novelist visiting London, marvelled at the glittering display of lamps in a Bedford Street shop, which included 'crystal, lacquer and metal ones, silver and brass in every shade'. Many of them were adapted, where possible, to hang from the ceiling; the Astral actually originated as a hanging lamp.

Robert Adam designed splendid brass hanging lamps for Osterley and other houses, and even more imposing, standard lamps with high bases in the classical style. But most remarkable of all was the great 30-spout bronze hanging lamp presented to the Royal Academy by the Prince Regent himself in 1812, which cost no less than £2,400. By the 1830s hanging gas lamps and chandeliers had begun to replace oil lamps in many rooms.

▲ *19th-century plain glass lamp with a bronze collar. Ornament is restricted to the decorative glass finial on the bottom.*

PRICE GUIDE **5**

▲ *Ruby-coloured glass hanging lamp which has lost the lid that would have been suspended above the bowl to keep smoke from damaging the ceiling. This should be reflected in the price.*

PRICE GUIDE **5**

▲ *An exotic-looking fluted blue glass lamp with an unusual and decorative arrangement of suspension chains, and handsome brass fittings.*

PRICE GUIDE **5**

PRICE GUIDE

Large numbers of oil lamps have survived and are still on the market, but the majority probably date from the Victorian period, when they were mass-produced to cater for the immense middle-class demand for table, portable, piano, reading and other lamps. The demand for oil lamps for the table continued unabated even after gas lights had replaced oil lamps for wall and ceiling lighting. Production was encouraged by the introduction of a new oil, paraffin, which was less liable to clog than colza oil, and which also rose up the wick by capillary action, making it possible to create a more discreet reservoir.

Regency lamps using colza oil – the Argand, Astral, Carcel and early Moderator – are less commonly found than Victorian ones and therefore fetch higher prices. The everyday brass version of the Argand lamp, sometimes known as a student's lamp, seems easy to identify because of its distinctive shape, with the lamp and opaque glass shade on one side of a central rod and the reservoir on the other. However, the stylishly workmanlike appearance resulting from this arrangement made it so popular that the design was used for many later paraffin models; so it should not be assumed that every Argand-style student's lamp was made during the Regency period. An alternative type, perhaps more suitable for the drawing room table, featured two burners, lamps and shades, one on each side of the reservoir; this created a pleasing symmetry and also minimized the problem of the shadow thrown by the reservoir.

LATER MODIFICATIONS

Many old oil lamps have been adapted to electricity. This offends some purists but is a positive advantage in the eyes of collectors who like to make their treasures a part of their way of life. In any case, lamps run on colza oil are not likely to be in working order, since burning this heavy fluid left thick deposits inside the burner which clogged the winding mechanism; most of them, twisted by impatient owners or their

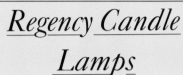

Regency Candle Lamps

EVEN THOUGH OIL LAMPS BECAME MUCH MORE WIDELY USED IN THE REGENCY ERA, MANY HOUSEHOLDS CONTINUED TO USE CANDLES AS A SUPPLEMENTARY FORM OF LIGHTING. HANGING LANTERNS, SUCH AS THE ONE SHOWN ON THE RIGHT, WERE POPULAR, ESPECIALLY FOR HALLS. FREE-STANDING CANDELABRA, LIKE THE BEAUTIFUL BRONZE AND ORMOLU EXAMPLE ON THE LEFT, COULD BE PLACED ON PEDESTALS, TABLES OR SIDEBOARDS.

Sheffield Plate Argand Lamp

ALTHOUGH IT IS UNMARKED, THIS SHEFFIELD PLATE TWO-LIGHT ARGAND LAMP WAS MADE BY MATTHEW BOULTON'S SOHO PLATE COMPANY IN BIRMINGHAM IN 1790. IT IS IN THE FORM OF A PLAIN COLUMN SUPPORTED ON A HALF-FLUTED DRUM; THE SPREADING BASE CONSISTS OF RADIATING FLUTES. THE LOWER HALF OF THE VASE-SHAPED CENTRAL OIL RESERVOIR IS DECORATED WITH CONCAVE FLUTING, AND THE STEPPED DOMED TOP HAS A SPHERICAL FINIAL. TWO CONCAVE FLUTED HORIZONTAL FAN-LIKE ARMS SUPPORT CYLINDRICAL BURNERS. THE CYLINDRICAL GLASS SHADES ARE UNDECORATED.

① AS IN ALL GRAVITY-FED OIL LAMPS, THE RESERVOIR IS PLACED HIGHER THAN THE BURNERS.

② THE ARMS ARE HOLLOW TO ALLOW THE OIL TO FLOW THROUGH.

③ AN ADJUSTER ENABLES THE CIRCULAR WICK TO BE RAISED OR LOWERED.

④ VENTILATION HOLES ARE AN ESSENTIAL FEATURE OF ALL OIL LAMPS.

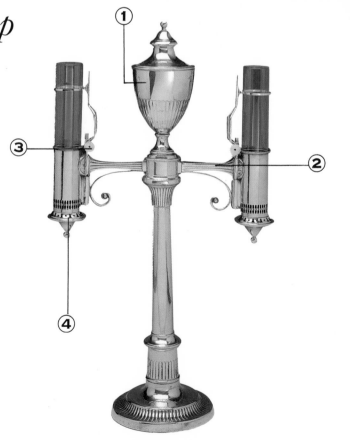

CLOSE UP

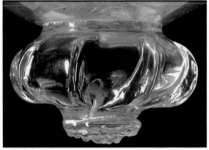

① BRONZE SWAG

③ GLASS FINIAL

⑤ WICK ADJUSTER

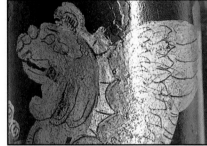

② LION'S HEAD MOTIF

④ HAND-PAINTED DETAILS

⑥ PINEAPPLE FINIAL

① THIS NEO-CLASSICAL BRONZE SWAG HAS BEEN FASTENED TO THE LAMP WITH SCREWS.

② A POPULAR DETAIL ON REGENCY FURNITURE, THIS LION'S HEAD DECORATES A LANTERN.

③ MANY 19TH-CENTURY HANGING OIL LAMPS HAVE DECORATIVE GLASS FINIALS.

④ GOLD PAINTED DETAILS ON A GREEN BACKGROUND ARE TYPICAL OF TÔLE WARE.

⑤ THIS WICK ADJUSTER IS STAMPED WITH THE NAME OF A PARISIAN MANUFACTURER.

⑥ THE GILDED METAL FINIAL ON THIS HANGING LAMP IS MADE IN THE FORM OF A PINEAPPLE.

servants, eventually snapped. Obviously, when confronted with any early lamp, it makes sense to check whether or not it works, or can be made to work.

Although often converted to electricity, the more ambitious or exotic Regency lamps are never cheap. Made of bronze, silver-plated, ebonized, gilded or mounted with ormolu, such aristocratic pieces generally pay lavish tribute to ancient Roman and Renaissance styles, their decoration often consisting of sculpted groups or reliefs, Corinthian columns, lions, cupids, garlands and other neo-classical elements.

CLASSICAL DECORATION

This was equally true of pottery lamps. By 1787, with his usual mixture of classicizing zeal and instinct for exploiting the latest technical innovation, Josiah Wedgwood was advertising 'lamps of two colours, adapted to Argand's patent lamp, the brilliant light of which being thrown on the bas-reliefs, has a singular and beautiful effect'. As well as upright lamps whose jasperware or basalt bases carried classical-style reliefs, Wedgwood also made delightful lamps in direct imitation of the boat-like ancient Roman originals, but with smooth neo-classical lines and the distinctly non-Roman white-on-blue colour scheme which

was so characteristic of his company's wares.

At the other extreme, crusie lamps, which are of great interest to the historically minded collector, can still be purchased. These are home-made iron lamps of the primitive open bowl type, used for centuries – and almost down to the present – in parts of Scotland and Ireland. The bowls are lozenge-shaped or oval, and the most distinctive crusies have two bowls, one above the other, the lower serving as a drip pan. Although they represent a link with the distant past, existing crusies are unlikely to go back beyond Regency times, since corrosion has destroyed earlier examples.

A final point worth remembering is that candles – and candle lamps – were also made during the Regency period, and indeed continued to be used right down to Edwardian times, either in combination with other forms of lighting or on their own. This was often an economy measure, since the solitary student found it cheaper to work by a single candle than to burn the proverbial midnight oil. For this purpose he or she could use a lamp with a glass funnel slotted into the body, which gave a constant light even in a draughty garret, or more sophisticated devices with hoods or screens that protected the eyes from the glare and concentrated the light on the page.

POINTS TO WATCH

■ Remember that some Regency designs were manufactured throughout the Victorian era, so check carefully for authenticity.

■ It is always worth ascertaining whether or not a lamp is in working order before you decide to buy.

■ There are some excellent modern reproductions available, so make sure you know whether or not you are buying an antique.

▲ *A highly ornate three-armed hanging lamp, which has been converted to electricity.*

Paperweights

Paperweights are made by hand and thus – with the exception of the simplest designs – no two are alike, so the possibilities for collections are infinite

There is an air of magic about paperweights. A good piece is unexpectedly heavy, and the images within the glass are illusory, delicate and beautiful.

The peak of refinement of paperweight making was surprisingly brief. The finest weights were made between 1842 and 1860, an era now known as the Classic period. The makers of individual weights, even the best, are usually unknown. The pieces these anonymous artesans made had little to do with other Victorian design elements, owing more to ancient decorative ideas. Paperweights were therefore accorded little status in Victorian eyes; recognition of their artistic value came much later.

A THOUSAND FLOWERS

It was the Alexandrians who first used 'millefiori' (a thousand flowers) designs in glass. Millefiori are made by placing rods of different coloured glass together, then heating and drawing them out to make slender canes. Each cane, viewed from its end, fancifully resembles a tiny flower, and many together look like a bed of flowers.

Millefiori surfaced again in Venice, probably in the 17th or 18th century. The first Venetian paperweights appeared in the early 1840s. Canes were covered in translucent glass in cylindrical, cubic or globular shapes. But the canes were just scrambled together and were left very near the surface of the weight.

It was left to others to discover the effect of arranging them carefully and covering them with a thick dome of clear glass. This magnified the canes and gave the pieces their resonant visual quality. The glassmakers of Bohemia may have been the first to perfect this technique. They were certainly producing weights at around the same time as the Venetians.

THE FRENCH MAKERS

By the mid-1840s the French had begun to produce fine paperweights which soon surpassed those from elsewhere.

The main factories in France during the Classic period were Baccarat, Saint Louis and Clichy. Baccarat and Saint Louis were located in the Vosges, and Clichy in Paris. They had in common a vein of very pure sand, essential to the manufacture of the highest quality glass.

These French glassmakers created millefiori weights of great complexity. In some the canes were arranged concentrically, in others they were placed in whirling groups. The canes themselves were often in the shape of stars, rings or wheels. Some of the most interesting are those with silhouettes of animals or of a little devil.

OTHER DESIGNS

Some paperweights included plants and animals of coloured glass. Pansies, reptiles, butterflies and dragonflies were great favourites. These were made by lampwork, sculpting the coloured glass over heat. The design was then reheated and covered in a dome of clear glass.

Another frequent element is 'latticino', in which fine threads of milky white glass are blown into elegant nets. These were often used to produce the effect of a basket around lampwork flowers and fruit. Alternatively, short lengths of net might be arranged to form muslin ground beneath coloured design elements. Latticino can also be in colours other than white.

Crown weights have twisted ribbons of coloured glass, perhaps interspersed with latticino ribbons, rising to a central flower. Twirl weights have strands

▼ *A selection of designs from different factories. This page, clockwise from bottom left: St Louis crown weight, c.1850; St Louis single pelargonium on a swirling latticino ground, c.1850; English round bubble weight, c.1880; northern English green glass stump, c.1880; French facetted sulphide of Napoleon III; Baccarat garlanded butterfly on muslin ground; Baccarat scattered millefiori on muslin ground with initial, date and silhouette canes, 1848; and Baccarat close millefiori with initial and date canes, 1848.*

of one or two colours plus white which rise in twirls to a central flower.

Sulphide paperweights have a ceramic medallion set in clear glass. The medallion often shows famous people such as Napoleon and Marie Antoinette, Victoria and Albert or, in the USA, American presidents.

Not all weights are globular. Some have facetted sides which provide multiple views of the central design. Overlay weights are facetted to provide windows on the design. To make an overlay, the clear glass weight was coated in one or more layers of coloured glass. This was then cut away in panels. The millefiori canes within the weight are often arranged in a mushroom shape.

Scramble weights are made of the tall-ends of millefiori canes which are simply jumbled together, rather than neatly arranged.

Millefiori were also used in other clear glass items to provide colour. They are most commonly found in ink bottles, both in the base and the stopper, and can also be seen in glass doorknobs.

FRENCH CHARACTERISTICS

It takes an expert eye to identify the makers of most paperweights. Very few French weights were either signed or dated.

Those that were contain canes bearing the date or the initial B, SL or C. Otherwise, variations between factories are subtle. Saint Louis weights were often in soft, muted colours; a number of Clichy weights contain a characteristic pink or white rose; and Baccarat weights, generally considered to be the finest of all, are often typified by the inclusion of starshaped canes. A distinctive star motif is often cut into the base of Baccarat weights; Clichy ones may have strawberry or square-cut bases.

ENGLISH MAKERS

From 1745 to 1845 English glassmaking was stifled by the harsh duty on glass. When this was lifted, English glass makers returned enthusiastically to the market. Paperweights were sold in stationers and 'fancy shops'. Customers could buy weights manufactured by Bacchus or Islington of Birmingham, or by Whitefriars of London. The best of the Bacchus weights were not far behind those made by the French masters. Millefiori were used, as were baskets of latticino, and canes were often characteristically arranged in an outer sheath around the central design.

COLLECTING PAPERWEIGHTS

A great paperweight revival got under way in the 1960s. The Americans, who had been making high quality weights from around the end of the Classic period onwards, helped to lead the way. Now makers there, in Britain, Italy and France – where Baccarat and Saint Louis have revived their great art – are producing fine weights.

Interesting limited editions are available from the

Baccarat with turquoise overlay

St Louis rose

Baccarat patterned millefiori

St Louis millefiori mushroom

Clichy pink dahlia-type

Clichy cross-ground concentric millefiori

Baccarat white carpet

St Louis pompon and pansy

St Louis mushroom, dated 1848

◀ Six quality floral paperweights from the three top French factories. Single flowers, particularly the rarer ones, are much sought-after and command some of the highest prices. Left to right from the top: Baccarat clematis with a star-cut base; Baccarat marguerite with a bud and a star-cut base; facetted St Louis bouquet within a torsade of white latticino; St Louis bouquet within a torsade of pink and white latticino; Clichy bouquet in a miniature weight; and a St Louis bouquet on a basket of white latticino.

▲ A sulphide, or cameo, paperweight made by Baccarat. In the best sulphides the cameo has a metallic look. This is a popular design, known as the huntsman, which was produced on a variety of coloured grounds and in clear glass. It was usually facetted, as here.

French makers, from British producers, such as Caithness, and from individual paperweight artists. Prices vary, but attractive weights can be found for under £30, though the best are considerably more.

Buying antique weights is perhaps rather different. Really high quality ones are rare and expensive, the best going for several thousand pounds. Other antique French weights fetch £200 upwards, depending on condition, beauty and rarity. There are fakes, too, so an expert's guidance should be sought.

Though they are robust antiques and easily looked after, paperweights can get damaged. When purchasing weights, those with chips or cracks should be avoided, as should those which have been ground down to remove faults, sometimes leaving the canes too near the surface. Weights with significant impurities or large bubbles obscuring the design or those with off-centre designs should also be avoided. Surface scratches do not reduce value.

Perhaps the best guide to purchasing paperweights is personal taste. A paperweight cannot be satisfactorily described; it must be weighed in the hand, turned and viewed. And when a fine paperweight is looked at like this, a potential investment is likely to turn into a permanent and much-loved drawing-room ornament.

·PRICE GUIDE· ANTIQUE PAPERWEIGHTS

At the top end of the market are the best French weights from the 1840s, notably those with double overlays or those containing rare single flowers, salamanders, snakes or insects. These can fetch from £4,000 to £10,000 plus. Other mid 19th-century weights, including elaborate English ones, French millefiori and early American, Italian and Bohemian weights will realize £400-£4,000.

Weights made this century in France by Paul Ysart (they contain a PY initialled cane) are valued in the hundreds.

From 1850 Kilner of Wakefield and other British bottle factories made green weights, some of which are actually doorstops. They often contain air bubbles which can be arranged in floral patterns. Others have glass flower-in-vase designs. These bottle-glass weights sell for £50-£300.

Victorian view weights, which have a sepia photograph of a tourist sight on the base, make an interesting collection at £10 to £50 each. At a similar price are 20th-century Chinese and Japanese weights, which have yellowish glass and crudely coloured canes.

There is little danger of confusing these oriental weights with more valuable western ones. However, there are French-made weights produced before the last War which can be passed off as or mistaken for Victorian weights. Paperweights by Dupont, which are now collected in their own right, can be confused with 19th-century Baccarat weights. The answer is to buy at auction or from a reputable dealer.

French Art Glass

The art glass manufacturers of Nancy combined technical experimentation with poetic conception to create a unique and original style

Extraordinarily fragile and yet malleable, glass was the medium that encapsulated the mood and ideals of *fin-de-siècle* France. Infinitely pliable in its hot molten state, no other medium was better suited to the sensuous, natural forms and the feeling of live, organic growth that characterize art nouveau design.

PAINTERLY EFFECTS

Hot or cold, glass could be blown, sculpted, carved, etched, decorated and chemically manipulated to achieve poetic and painterly effects. The repertoire of these effects was hugely expanded in the late 19th century, when the debased aesthetic standards of industrial products encouraged certain designers to place a special premium on craftsmanship and manufacture by hand.

Today, the appeal of French art glass lies in its combination of virtuoso technique and poetic conception, and for collectors it has a special cachet: although most makers produced several copies of each model, chemical reactions and hand manufacture mean that no two vessels are ever identical.

Most of the glass was made in Nancy, the provincial capital of Lorraine, and at glassworks in the Parisian suburbs. It was Nancy, significantly, that emerged as the prime focus of art nouveau design after the defeat of France during the Franco-

Chinese Cased Glass

CAMEO OR CASED GLASS WAS INVENTED IN ANTIQUITY, AND THIS CHINESE CASED GLASS BOTTLE DATES TO THE 18TH CENTURY — JUST OVER 100 YEARS BEFORE EMILE GALLÉ REVIVED THE TECHNIQUE IN FRANCE.

Prussian War of 1870-71. While much of north-east Lorraine was ceded to Germany, Nancy remained French – retaining the pride and energy for a cultural revolution.

A Gathering Of Talents

Diverse creative talents gathered there, including well-known metalworkers and furniture designers like Louis Majorelle and Edgar Brandt. But the leading spirit was the glass designer Emile Gallé. He fostered a spirit of cooperative production and mutual support, even though his own glassworks were in competition with large manufacturers like Daum, established in 1875, and Muller Frères at nearby Lunéville. Many of the Nancy craftsmen and

▶ *This view inside the Gallé glassworks shows craftsmen at work on the firm's vases. They are painting certain areas of the glass with bitumen to prevent them being eaten away during the acid etching process. Many of Gallé's industrial pieces were acid-etched rather than engraved by hand because this technique was faster and adapted well to mass-production.*

◀ *Three distinctive vases sit on an inlaid wooden table designed by Gallé. Each represents one of the leading manufacturers of the Nancy School: the vase with a green seascape on the left is by Muller Frères; the one in the middle with toadstools set against a streaked background is by Daum; and on the right is a Gallé cameo vase whose shape reflects oriental inspiration.*

technicians, including the Mullers, were trained by, or collaborated with, Gallé.

Gallé's lofty mission was 'to calm men' through the solace of art and nature, and nature was a sourcebook for the unique and original Nancy style. Motifs were culled from the rich flora and fauna of the Lorraine countryside, or from the huge range of botanical specimens cultivated by Gallé in his own garden. Designers usually worked with the model in front of them. Apart from the familiar dragonfly and butterfly, humble species became favourite subjects: mosses, wild grasses and cereals, poppies, cornflowers, mistletoe, fungi, toads, bats, moths and beetles. Conventional shapes gave way to lamps and vases modelled as mushrooms, ripe gourds, onion bulbs, fragile stems, or the corolla of a flower. The purity and economy of Japanese art was also an inspiration. About 75 per cent of Gallé's shapes were adapted from the vessels used for Japanese cultural ceremonies like tea drinking and flower arranging.

Poetic Forms

Although goblets, plates and other items of tableware were manufactured, the quintessential art glass object was the vase – no mere container, but a 'sculpture' and a vehicle for philosophy and sentiment. From 1884, Gallé created *verrerie parlante* ('speaking glass'), much of it inscribed with poignant lines of poetry from Baudelaire and Victor Hugo, which encapsulate the melancholy lyricism of art nouveau.

Poetry was also evoked through the abstract means of colour, iridescence and texture. Experiments with metallic oxides, fumes, impurities and firing techniques enabled special effects like *craquelure*

(cracking), pearls and gas bubbles, and patinas, to suggest seasonal moods and atmospheres.

In the early years, art glass was only collected by museums, dandies and aesthetes like Comte Robert de Montesquiou and Marcel Proust. But by the 1890s a large enough market existed for the Gallé and Daum factories to employ 300 workers each, and Gallé opened shops in Paris, Frankfurt and London. Acid etching, rather than the time-consuming wheel engraving, facilitated bulk production, and mass-produced industrial vessels were made alongside the luxury limited editions. However, it was only after public demand was stimulated by the International Exhibition of 1900 that the full commercial potential of art glass was realised.

Mass Production for Export

In 1901, in order to compete with foreign makers and very large Parisian firms like Legras et Cie, Gallé formalized the Lorraine group into the *Ecole de Nancy* (Nancy School). Their first communal exhibition was mounted in 1903 at the Louvre in Paris. But within a year, Gallé had died of leukaemia, and in the decade leading up to World War I the Nancy school began to suffer from creative stagnation, which was compounded by the lure of cheap, mass production for lucrative export markets.

Gallé's mission was betrayed by declining industrial standards and cheapened sentiment, and by the 1920s, modernists had already condemned art nouveau as the product of a diseased and decadent aestheticism. For four decades, art glass remained a target for scorn and abuse.

Emile Gallé Glass

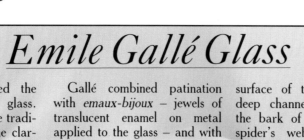

Gallé revolutionized the manufacture of glass. Going against the traditional quest for crystalline clarity, he deliberately sought effects of opacity, iridescence, saturated colour, *craquelure*, internal 'flaws' and surface texture more typical of metals, minerals and natural stones. For patination, he turned a technical hazard (contaminating wood and coal dust in the furnace) into an aesthetic triumph, using these impurities to give the glass surface the quality of a fabric or the ability to suggest mist, rain and other atmospheric effects.

Gallé combined patination with *emaux-bijoux* – jewels of translucent enamel on metal applied to the glass – and with his unique 'marquetry', a technique that came close to painting. Sheets or fragments of glass were inserted into the hot mass in single or superimposed layers, intensifying the colour. Gallé's most complicated vases were constructed of several separately coloured 'cases' or layers of glass, wheel-engraved to different depths revealing each layer below, and finished with marquetry and patination. Gallé also used acid to bite into the

surface of the glass, creating deep channels which imitated the bark of a tree, or a fine spider's web of lines which captured the fragility of an insect's wing.

▶ *A pink and green vase from 1910, decorated with acorns and leaves.*

PRICE GUIDE **7**

▼ *Very large bowl from 1906-7, with brown overlay on an opaline ground depicting a tranquil riverscape.*

PRICE GUIDE **8**

▶ *A delicate tracery of yellow honeysuckle flowers with brown stems and leaves plays over the surface of this vase.*

PRICE GUIDE **8**

PRICE GUIDE

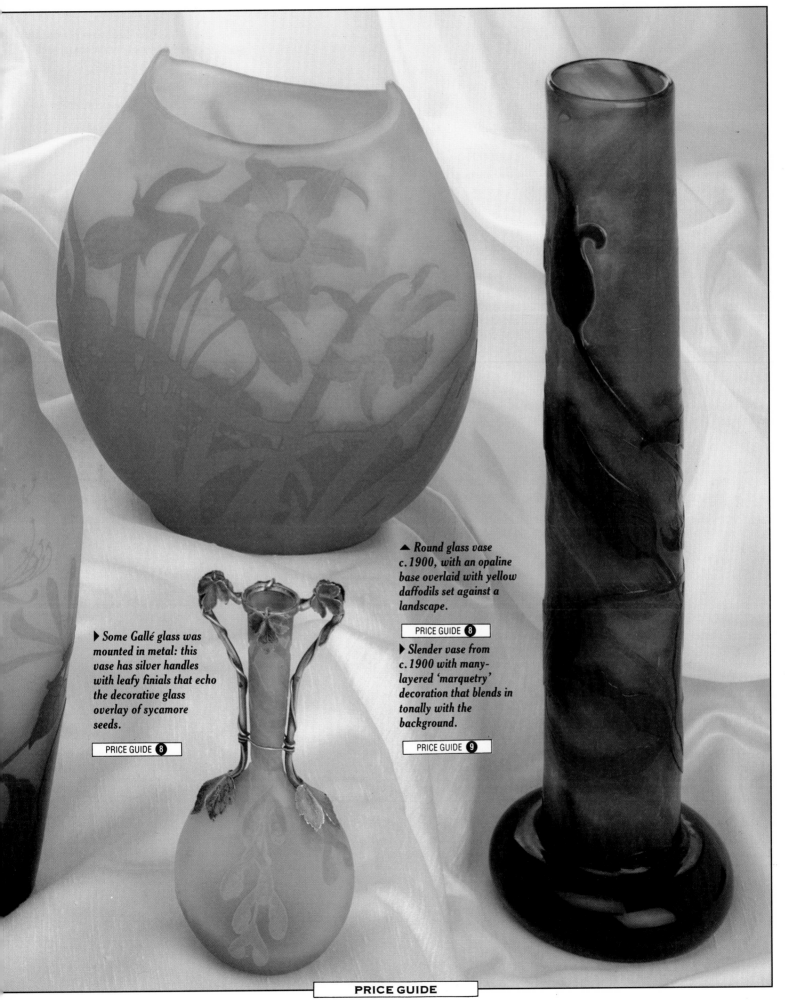

▲ Round glass vase c. 1900, with an opaline base overlaid with yellow daffodils set against a landscape.

PRICE GUIDE **8**

▶ Some Gallé glass was mounted in metal: this vase has silver handles with leafy finials that echo the decorative glass overlay of sycamore seeds.

PRICE GUIDE **8**

▶ Slender vase from c. 1900 with many-layered 'marquetry' decoration that blends in tonally with the background.

PRICE GUIDE **9**

PRICE GUIDE

Daum and Muller Glass

The firm of Daum was established in 1875, but only moved into art glass production after 1887, inspired by Gallé's success. Daum products have a distinctive mottled, streaked or shaded appearance, achieved by mixing powdered glass and additives into the glass during smelting. The beautiful dusky shades of green, violet and orange were well suited to the lamps that Daum manufactured from 1900, the richness of the technique responding to internal illumination. Daum is also renowned for *berluzes* or bulbous vases with very long, thin necks based on 6th and 7th century Persian bottles, and for 'intercalary' or multi-layered cameo vases with surfaces carved to reveal further layers of engraved, etched and enamelled glass below.

The Muller brothers, who trained with Gallé, set up their business in 1895. Their vases, sometimes combining up to seven coloured layers of glass, are distinguished by excellent carving. A special Muller technique was *fluogravure*, which used hydrofluoric acid to bite into glass painted with intensely coloured or iridescent enamels. Among landscape and floral motifs, they occasionally applied glass cabochons carved as insects. Muller glass also responded well to internal illumination and was popular for lamps and light fittings which exploited this potential.

▼ This Daum vase from c.1900 has been acid-etched with orange and green flowers.

PRICE GUIDE **8**

▲ A Muller Frères vase with characteristic mottled background overlaid with purple and yellow crocuses and a grasshopper.

PRICE GUIDE **8**

▼ An oblong Daum vase whose shape betrays Japanese inspiration. The fuchsias have been applied with enamel paint.

PRICE GUIDE **7**

▲ An unusual Daum vase with gold and white mistletoe overlay and a gold rim.

PRICE GUIDE **6**

▶ Squat rectangular Daum vase with a panoramic landscape showing a river and trees.

PRICE GUIDE **7**

▲ Round blue Daum vase from around 1900, with peacock feather cameo decoration.

PRICE GUIDE **8**

PRICE GUIDE

▼ *Muller Frères ball-shaped vase from c. 1900, decorated with an alpine landscape showing a lake framed by mountains and trees.*

PRICE GUIDE **9**

▲ *Daum bowl with enamel-painted apple blossom set against cream and peach background.*

PRICE GUIDE **8**

▶ *Elongated Daum vase with a tangle of yellow flowers painted on to a yellow and mauve streaked background.*

PRICE GUIDE **8**

PRICE GUIDE

COLLECTOR'S TIPS

Daum and Gallé vases are no longer as cheap as they once were. Heavy investment by Far Eastern collectors has pushed up prices enormously, and many of the finest pieces have been exported.

Signed, limited edition pieces will be beyond the price range of most collectors, but 'industrial' (mass-produced) glass can still be bought for more reasonable prices. The umbrella term 'industrial' can embrace everything from artistic acid-etched cameo glass to mould-blown pieces with stencilled decoration, but as far as Gallé glass is concerned, it generally means an acid-etched vessel of one, two or three layers, without any complicated additional techniques such as marquetry or metallic occlusions. Accessible and popular examples include the two-colour red/yellow and blue/yellow vases etched on the outer and inner surfaces.

Industrial pieces from the 1890s and early 1900s, when Gallé was designing for mass-production, are certainly worth collecting since commercial, modest-budget glass was as integral to his business and his philosophy as the more exclusive 'artistic' models. After Gallé's death, however, standards declined and industrial glass from the 1920s tends to be marred by repetitive design, weak colour and a loss of definition and detail. Gallé's strong blues and reds were often dropped in favour of dull browns and greens (iron oxides were cheaper than cobalt and uranium oxide), and the impurities in inferior quality glass resulted in gas bubbles. The collector should try to avoid pieces which contain flaws such as these.

For different budgets there is a vast range between the industrial vase, and the rare model of technical perfection, with documentation, provenance or a special inscription. Prices are based on an assessment of artistic conception, rarity, technique, the number of layers of glass, shape, colour and subject matter. This requires experience and an expert eye, and the best advice is to stick to a reputable dealer since the pitfalls are numerous.

BEWARE OF LATER ALTERATIONS

Glass is fairly easy to shave, so chipped feet and rims are sometimes cut down, undermining the properties of the vessel. There are numerous vases on the market with amputated necks and feet – even lamp bases that have become vases, and vases that have become bowls. To the uninitiated eye, however, this surgery may not be all that easy to spot, especially since a large number of art nouveau shapes were adapted from Japanese models and may look unfamiliar anyway. Examples are the squat 'tea ceremony' bowls and straight-necked vases for flower arranging (some were 'Europeanized' with a curved rim, some were not).

Damage and modern repair with plastic or resin are not noted in sale catalogue

Tiffany Glass

WHILE GALLÉ, DAUM AND MULLER WERE CREATING NEW FORMS OF GLASS IN FRANCE, IN AMERICA LOUIS COMFORT TIFFANY WAS DEVELOPING HIS 'FAVRILE' GLASS WITH ITS CHARACTERISTIC IRIDESCENT SURFACES AND GENTLE RAINBOW HUES.

Gallé Syrian Vase

EARLY ON IN HIS CAREER, GALLÉ DEVELOPED A FASCINATION FOR ISLAMIC GLASS, AND HE ADOPTED ITS SWIRLING LINES, FLAT, ORNAMENTAL FOLIAGE AND BRILLIANT ENAMEL COLOURS FOR SOME OF HIS OWN PIECES. THE SHAPE OF THIS VASE, WITH ITS NARROW NECK AND TWO HANDLES, IS REMINISCENT OF THE ANCIENT MEDITERRANEAN AMPHORA, AND ITS DECORATION CONTAINS STRONG ECHOES OF ISLAMIC PATTERNS. PIECES LIKE THIS ARE, HOWEVER, RELATIVELY SCARCE, SINCE GALLÉ WAS NOT SATISFIED FOR LONG WITH IMITATING ANTIQUE PROTOTYPES, AND SOON MOVED ON TO CREATE HIS OWN DISTINCTIVE SERIES OF STYLES.

① FOLLOWING THE ARABIC METHOD, GALLÉ HAS APPLIED HARD ENAMEL COLOURS TO THE SURFACE OF THE GLASS.

② THE BLOBS OF PAINT THAT STAND OUT IN RELIEF ANTICIPATE GALLÉ'S LATER MODELLED PIECES.

③ THE CURVILINEAR DECORATION SHOWS A CLEAR DEBT TO ISLAMIC PATTERNS.

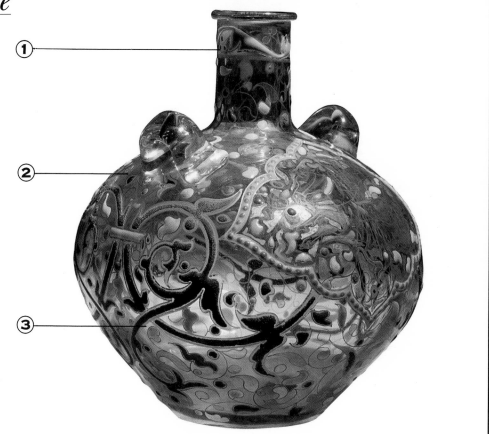

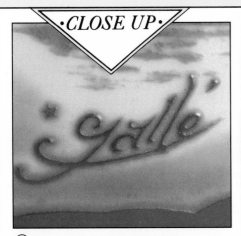

·CLOSE UP·

① GALLÉ SIGNATURE AND STAR

② DAUM SIGNATURE

③ MULLER FRÈRES SIGNATURE

④ GRACEFUL FLOWERS

⑤ SILVER MOUNT

⑥ ENAMEL-PAINTED FLOWER

① A GALLÉ SIGNATURE WITH THE ADDITION OF A STAR INDICATES A PIECE COMPLETED AFTER GALLÉ'S DEATH IN 1904.

④ GALLÉ DELIGHTED IN THE GRACE OF FLOWERS, AND DETAILS SUCH AS THIS DAFFODIL SHOW HOW CLOSELY HE OBSERVED NATURE.

② THE DAUM SIGNATURE IS USUALLY ACCOMPANIED BY THE CROSS OF LORRAINE – A TRIBUTE TO THE INDEPENDENT SPIRIT OF THE PROVINCE.

⑤ GALLÉ OFTEN HAD THE BRONZE AND SILVER MOUNTS FOR HIS PIECES MADE IN HIS OWN STUDIO SO THAT THEY COMPLEMENTED THE GLASS.

③ THE PRE-1914 SIGNATURE INCLUDED THE WORDS 'CROISMARE PRÈS NANCY'. AFTER 1919 THIS WAS REPLACED WITH 'LUNÉVILLE'.

⑥ THIS FLOWER, PAINTED IN BRILLIANTLY VIBRANT ENAMEL COLOURS, STANDS OUT CLEARLY AGAINST THE MOTTLED BACKGROUND.

descriptions, so it is easy to pay over the odds at auction for imperfect pieces. Fake or substitute signatures and outright forgeries are a further hazard. Imitation Gallé vases are currently being manufactured in France and are acquiring fake signatures elsewhere, and only specialist dealers are likely to notice minor discrepancies in colour and shape – although occasionally there are more obvious blunders, like blue cherry blossom!

RARITY AND CRAFTSMANSHIP

Elegant shapes, strong colours and characteristic art nouveau motifs like the butterfly and dragonfly all increase the value of a piece. Its price will also reflect rarity, technical accomplishment and the degree of craftsmanship – the more expensive pieces having applied or intercalary decoration,

cabochons, metal occlusions, patination and wheel carving rather than (or as well as) acid etching. Gallé's marquetry vases are much prized, since this high-risk technique (nine of every ten attempts were destroyed) was not continued after his death.

POINTS TO WATCH

■ Look for vessels with an overall harmony of design, subject and technique, and a poetic conception characteristic of the era.

■ Damaged 'industrial' vessels are valueless, but imperfect, rare models by top designers may be worth collecting. Gallé's damaged and unfinished pieces, stamped 'étude' (study), are an example.

■ Hand-made pieces are a more worthwhile investment than mass-produced onces.

■ Stick to a reputable dealer, and ask for advice on damage, repair, and signatures.

▲ *Glass could be put to the most ingenious uses. This oval, with a central bouquet of flowers surrounded by a gold border, is actually one of a set of French buttons dating from the turn of the century.*

Jugendstil Glass

The Jugendstil glassmakers' experimentation with shapes and decoration resulted in a brief but brilliant flowering of glass design

In an era of commercialism, mass-production and loss of originality, Jugendstil glass was radically different, standing for individuality, craftsmanship and novelty. It explored new and unexpected shapes and developed novel effects by exploiting a range of neglected decorative techniques.

Jugendstil glass was made mainly in the 30 years leading up to 1900, in Austria, Germany and the Habsburg Empire. As the Germanic equivalent of French art nouveau, Jugendstil was similarly applied to all forms of manufacturing craftsmanship, from furniture to ceramics. It was, however, in glassware that Jugendstil found its most eloquent expression.

Bohemia had long been an important centre of glass-making. Indeed, the region had been famous for its coloured glass and enamelled glassware in the 16th, 17th and 18th centuries. In the 19th century, Germany produced clear, stained and overlay glass decorated with finely painted scenes and delicate engraving. By the late 19th century, however, this artistry had been replaced with stagnation and repetition. Shapes were trapped in the straitjacket of stereotype and symmetry, and the glass itself decorated as if it were porcelain.

A RETURN TO EXPERIMENTATION

Consciously overturning this state of affairs, craftsmen working in the Jugendstil tradition returned to experimentation with the very nature of glass, its translucent effects and its malleability when molten. Originality and artistry were the order of the day; the function of a bowl or vase soon became secondary to its interesting shape, fascinating iridescence or unexpected etched, enamelled or applied decoration.

Some Jugendstil glass took slender, elegant and symmetrical shapes. At the height of the style, however, interesting, asymmetrical shapes were produced by hand-shaping the molten glass, twisting, pinching and pulling it into original and unusual forms. Bowls could be pinched in at the waist or rim, and the necks of vases pulled and twisted into undulating 'goose-neck' attitudes and the plant-like forms that are so typical of art nouveau.

A range of decorative techniques came into their

▶ *This selection of Jugendstil glass includes a number of pinched, twisted and moulded designs in iridescent colours, a large vase with a silver and gold peacock feather design, a few pieces of clear, painted glass and a small vase with an applied silver metal design.*

own. Iridescent glassware became particularly prominent. Iridescence, which appears naturally on glass that has been buried for long periods, was seen on Roman glass that was being excavated at the time. The same effects could be produced by coating glass with metallic oxides and heating it in the furnace. Gold oxide produced a ruby lustre, silver a yellow lustre, and platinum, silvery reflections. Copper (for green), bismuth and uranium oxides were also used.

Cased glass, made of two or more layers of different coloured glass, and cameo glass, in which the outer layer of cased glass was carved or acid-etched, were also important. Both had been used earlier in the 19th century but, in the hands of Jugendstil craftsmen, both acquired exciting new design aspects.

Combed decoration, another technique used by Jugendstil glassmakers, was achieved by adding threads of coloured glass to a molten 'gather' and dragging them across the surface to produce festoons and marbled patterns. Interesting effects were also produced by glassware that imitated hardstones such as onyx and aventurine.

▲ *This exquisite vase from the Moser school features ground windows and a blue cased chestnut leaf design.*

LOETZ GLASS

The firm of Loetz, of Klostermühle, one of the best-known Austrian glassworks, played a leading role in the production of Jugendstil glass. During the 1880s, the factory produced glassware that imitated onyx, cornelian, agate, chalcedony, aventurine, jasper and other hardstones. It is, however, for the iridescent glassware made between about 1890 and 1900 that Loetz is justly famous.

There were two main types of Loetz iridescent glass: 'Papillon', consisting of pearly spots covering a vessel, and 'Phenomenon', with glass threads undulating across a pearly surface. Loetz's best pieces of iridescent glassware are sumptuous in colour and sensuous in form. Among the more novel shapes are twisted, pinched and goose-neck vases, three-handled vessels and pieces with applied decoration in the form of snakes. Some vases were mounted in silver, bronze or other metals.

Much of Loetz's iridescent glassware was made in imitation of the American Louis Comfort Tiffany's Favrile glass. Loetz glass also crossed the Atlantic and was sold alongside Tiffany's products, bearing a Loetz factory mark to distinguish it from Tiffany glass, as the two could appear very similar.

It was in fact the firm of J & L Lobmeyr that had pioneered the commercial production of iridescent glass in the 1860s. By the turn of the century, however, Lobmeyr's strength lay in finely engraved, enamelled or gilt glassware designed by some of the most original artists in Austria.

For J & L Lobmeyr, the designer Josef Hoffman developed 'bronzitdecor', a new type of decoration consisting of geometric lines and floral motifs painted in black or grey on clear or matt glass.

▲ *Attributed to Kolo Moser, this vase has two blue-green 'eyes' mounted onto the glass, which has been dyed pink and gilded with metallic finishes.*

ARTISTS' ORIGINAL DESIGNS

From the late 19th century, artists such as Josef Maria Olbrich, Otto Prutscher, Rudolf Bakalowitz and Koloman Moser, together with members of the Vienna School of Arts and Crafts, worked to commission for the Viennese firm of E Bakalowitz & Söhne. Their original designs were executed by various Bohemian factories, including Loetz. Among these commissions were iridescent glassware in various lustres, bronze-mounted vases and crystal candlesticks, and a range of long-stemmed wine glasses and decanters in overlaid transparent glass.

Highly regarded at the turn of the century, although little known today, was the firm of Harrach. The factory's products included direct copies of Tiffany vases, cameo and cased glass and, of course, iridescent glass.

Ludwig Moser & Sons, of Karlsbad, concentrated on carved and cameo glass. Most characteristic of the factory's products were boldly shaped cases in purple glass decorated with gilt plants or figures, and carved and etched pieces overlaid in green and purple. The iris was a recurring motif.

Iridescent glass, meanwhile, had become extremely popular and, taking advantage of demand, many other glass-making concerns in Austria, Germany and Bohemia took up its manufacture. Among the lesser factories were Heckert, Pallme Konig, Kralik, Goldberg and Adolf Zasche.

THE END OF JUGENDSTIL GLASS

The flowering of Jugendstil cameo and iridescent glassware was sadly short-lived. By 1900, the glossy iridescence and intriguing play of colours in cameo glass that had been perfected over the last 30

◀ Jugendstil glass incorporated metal in a variety of ways, including applied silverwork in geometrical and natural designs, gold dust which has been trapped within layers of glass and the addition of metal handles, stands and rims.

▼ The colours, patterns and iridescence which make Jugendstil glassware so outstanding and collectable are displayed in this striking collection of elegant and unusual vases.

years was beginning to be rejected in favour of starker, simpler colour contrasts. Shapes lost their free-blown irregularity, and greater simplicity in etching and enamelling became established.

Jugendstil glassware is generally recognizable by its slender forms and rich iridescence or applied or cased decoration. It is generally more delicate than French art nouveau glassware, and is also rarer.

The quality of Jugendstil glassware, including that made by such major names as Loetz and Lobmeyr, ranges from superb to undistinguished. Cased and cameo pieces are rarer than iridescent vases, which were made in the largest numbers and are thus the most frequently seen today. A quantity of them are unmarked, and while some can be ascribed to the more important factories, the individual products of lesser factories are difficult to identify.

Across the range, Jugendstil glass is valued according to manufacturer, and the individual designer where this is known. Generally, the most highly valued Jugendstil glassware is that made by either Lobmeyr or Loetz, followed by that produced

by F Heckert and Harrach. A signature can add to the value of a piece; much Loetz glass is unsigned, but 'Loetz Austria' or 'Lötz, Klostermühle' will be seen on some pieces.

The cachet of a signature should not blind a buyer to the real value of a piece. An anonymous piece of good design may be a better buy than a signed but unremarkable vase by a prestigious factory.

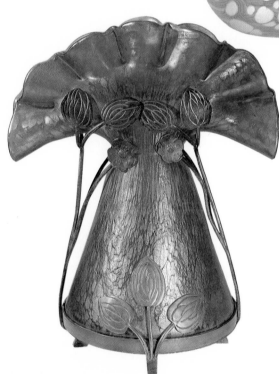

▲ A Loetz vase, typical of the delicate and innovative designs of the period, decorated with silvery iridescent splashes.

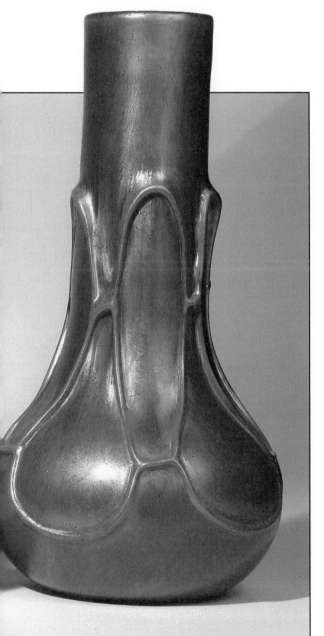

◀ This 'Papillon' iridescent vase, again from the Loetz Glassworks, has a fan-shaped edge and is mounted in a gilded bronze plant-shaped design.

·PRICE GUIDE· JUGENDSTIL GLASS

Prices for the plainest and unattributed pieces of Jugendstil glass start at about £25-£30. A drinking glass by a major manufacturer can command prices up to about £60.

Cameo and enamelled vases, together with iridescent glassware by lesser or unknown factories, are generally priced in the region of £250-

£400. Allowance should also be made for rarity and quality.

Across the range, the products of Loetz and Lobmeyr are the most highly priced. Iridescent vases command £300 at their cheapest. Prices can double for signed pieces. A top-quality, signed vase may command anything up to about £10,000.

Bohemian Glass

During the Biedermeier period the craftsmen and factories of Bohemia began creating new types of glass that appealed to the growing middle classes

Since the 15th century Bohemia has had one of Europe's richest traditions in glassware. Bohemia is one of the three major divisions of what is now Czechoslovakia. For most of its period as a great glass-making centre, however, Bohemia was part of the Habsburg Empire, whose capital was Vienna.

It was a momentous time for the Bohemian glass industry, which underwent a period of near collapse and then revival. In the 18th century Bohemian cut and engraved glass had led the world in its originality of design, profusion of motifs and richness of ornamentation. However at the end of the century it lost its pre-eminence, as English lead glass became highly fashionable and at the same time the Napoleonic Wars had a disastrous effect on Europe's economy. After the end of the wars in 1815, however, the determination of Bohemian glassmakers to regain their dominance brought about the second great age of Bohemian glass – the Biedermeier age.

BIG BUSINESS

Although this was the period of the Industrial Revolution and the beginning of mass production, many Bohemian glass factories retained their links with the past. They were still largely family firms, operating independently and generally burning wood rather than coal in their furnaces. Overall, though, it was a very big business – at the beginning of the 19th century there were 66 glass factories in Bohemia employing some 40,000 people.

The variety of artefacts that these factories turned out was enormous. Beakers, vases, phials, chandeliers and drinking glasses were made for practical use, but great quantities of purely decorative items were also produced. In particular an enormous market in glass souvenirs grew up in fashionable spas such as Carlsbad, Marienbad, Teplitz and Baden.

GLASS ENGRAVERS

One of the first of the great Bohemian glassmakers to capitalize on the tourist trade was the engraver, Dominik Biemann. Each season he would set up a workshop at the fashionable spa of Franzensbad and engrave portraits and landscapes on commission. Far from cheap souvenirs, these pieces were beautifully executed works in a neo-classical style, made for the newly rich middle classes who were prepared to pay large sums for such fine objects.

▲ *Made around 1830, this goblet has a ruby bowl with an amber flash panel depicting a hunting scene.*

◀ *From the left, clockwise: a green glass deckelpokal with stag engraving, made of Annagrün glass in about 1850; a clear glass deckelpokal made around 1840; a deckelpokal with engraved hunting scene, made around 1840; and a rose-coloured deckelpokal with transparent stem, made around 1850.*

Other notable engravers of the period were Karl Pfohl, Mattoni of Carlsbad and the families of Moser, Pelikan of Meisterdorf and Simms of Gablonz. They executed a variety of designs including horses, mountaineers with ropes, children at play, public buildings, palaces and views. Often a sentimental message was also engraved on such keepsakes. Some of this work was signed although often equally fine pieces were left unsigned.

PAINTED DECORATION

The invention of painting in transparent rather than opaque enamel colours resulted in far greater detail and sensitivity in the painted decoration of glass. Samuel Mohn introduced this new technique in 1811 on his arrival in Vienna. He painted simple, naturalistic landscapes, cities and churches. But his son, Gottlöb, was in the forefront of the new romantic style in pastorals and sentimental allegories that appealed to middle-class taste.

Romanticism was a hugely influential force in all areas of art and design during this period. It also produced the new enthusiasm for looking at landscapes and visiting places of natural beauty, which in turn fuelled the souvenir market.

One of the most successful of these souvenir glass painters was Anthon Kothgasser (1769-1851) of Vienna, who was already well known as a porcelain painter when he turned his attention to glass. He painted portraits, genre scenes, moonlit views and

◀ *From the top, clockwise: a wine goblet made in about 1850; a wine glass dating from about 1840; a glass beaker from the late 1850s, engraved by Pfohl; and an engraved goblet from around 1850.*

▲ *A faceted goblet in glass and gilt, c. 1818.*

▲ *A deckelpokal (goblet and cover) with an engraving by Borg Böhn, made in 1838.*

mann, who also produced objects in hyalith glass, and then in 1823 came up with a variety of glass which he called *lithyalin*. This was a marbled glass which embodied an extraordinary variety of colours, ranging from brick red streaked with green to deep blues and purples.

Egermann was also responsible for developing a 'gold' stain that Kothgasser often used as a background to his paintings and for finding a way of replacing gold with copper in the manufacture of ruby glass.

SHADES OF URANIUM

During the 1830s the continuing search for novelty produced a variety of new colours in glass by the addition of the metallic elements antimony and uranium to the copper. Turquoise, topaz and chrysoprase were added to the glassworkers' palette, as well as two shades of uranium green, each named by their originator, Joseph Riedel, after his wife Anna as 'Annagrün' and 'Annagelb'.

Other techniques employed by the Bohemian glassmakers of the period included stained glass, where clear glass is given surface colours of vivid reds, greens and yellows, as well as gold and silver. A process secret to Bohemia until the 1850s was overlay or cased glass, in which a glass object was encased in opaque or different coloured glass, and then cut away to reveal the contrasting layer beneath.

Until 1848, when revolution upset the placid and prosperous world of the middle classes throughout much of Europe, Bohemian glass reigned supreme both at the expensive and the cheap end of the market. The greatest artists worked to order for private clients, while copies of their work of varying quality were mass-produced for export and domestic markets. The collector will find generally that glass produced after about 1850 shows a marked deterioration both in design and execution.

COLLECTING BIEDERMEIER GLASS

Many of the finest examples of Biedermeier glass are seen only in museums, but good work can still be found in antique shops. Signed work is particularly desirable, though not common, and a great number of extremely high quality pieces were not signed. Very few really top quality pieces come on to the market – perhaps two or three a year will be sold by the major auction houses.

illustrations of proverbs, all of which are characterized by his superb technique and attention to detail.

Kothgassen is credited with the introduction of that most characteristic of Biedermeier designs, the *Ranftbecher*. This was a trumpet-shaped beaker with a heavy foot which was often facet-cut. As well as a painted scene on its tapering body, the beaker would usually be finished with transparent enamelling or gilding on the rim and base.

Some of Kothgasser's paintings on glass give an indication of the kind of people who were buying this glassware. On one beaker the affluent and confident bourgeoisie of early 19th-century Vienna are pictured strolling and conversing in front of the magnificent St Stephen's Cathedral – the middle classes at play. Another Ranftbecher features an allegorical scene of bees and a hive, symbolizing bourgeois attitudes to the importance of hard work and industry.

PERIOD OF INNOVATION

The Biedermeier age was a period of enormous innovation in the manufacture of glass. In 1822 the southern Bohemian glasshouses of Count George Buquoy created a dense, black glass which he called *hyalith*. This was designed to imitate the popular black basaltes of Wedgwood. There was also a red version similar to Wedgwood's *rosso antico*.

Another notable innovator was Friedrich Eger-

Spoons

Spoons have been around for centuries and their varying designs and materials offer plenty of scope for those wanting to form a collection

For hundreds of years people carried their own spoons, which were as personal an item as a pocketwatch. Today they make ideal collectors' items as they are small, useful, and not necessarily expensive. The basic shape and design of the spoon has evolved over centuries, with long periods of overlap between styles. Dates given here are for their heyday.

FIVE CENTURIES OF DESIGN

Medieval spoons had rounded or fig-shaped bowls and thin metal bars, square or hexagonal in section, for handles, or steles. The best were made of silver, though brass and pewter were more common.

Two spoons were generally made from a small ingot. The ends were teased into bowls and the ingot was cut in the middle, usually at an angle; this provided a surface large enough for the owner's initials to be engraved. Alternatively, a small decorative cast-metal piece called a knop was soldered to the stele. Early knops were in the shape of balls, lozenges and acorns. Figures were introduced in the 16th century.

The most popular figure knops were saints. Each was identified by his emblem – a cup for John, keys for Peter, and so on. These have become known as apostle spoons, though many other saints are represented, and the best apostle spoons are 16th century; later spoons use the same moulds but these became coarse with use.

In the course of the 17th century, spoons went from being luxury items to more or less everyday objects. There were no stylistic changes – save for a lengthening of the steles to accommodate the fashion for ruffled collars – until the Commonwealth, when a radical new design, the Puritan spoon, emerged. The stele became a flattened handle and was attached to a heavy, elliptical bowl. The handle was cut off square at the end, with two or three filed notches as the only decoration.

Knops returned with the monarchy, but the practical advantages of the Puritan spoon were retained in the trefid (or *pied de biche*) spoon that was the main style for the rest of the century. It was characterized by a three-lobed terminal to the handle, while the line of the handle was continued under the bowl in a rat-tail. The handle turned down at the bowl and up at the end, as it was the custom to lay tables with the spoon bowl facing downwards. The underside of the bowls and the handles were often embossed with a lacework design or engraved all over with foliage.

In the reign of Queen Anne, the two outer lobes of

the terminal disappeared, giving a transitional style called dognose. Around 1715 this gave way to the simple rounded ends of the Hanoverian style. Although the rat-tails survived to the middle of the century, they began to be replaced by a simpler strengthening called a drop.

From 1730 on, spoons began to be laid bowl up, which meant the end of the handle turned down; both styles were made throughout the century. Those spoons that were turned down and lacked the central ridge along the handle, which characterized the

▲ *It is small wonder that caddy spoons are so eagerly collected; they come in such elegant designs. Silver is the most usual material but the four spoons at top left illustrate alternatives. From the top: copper gilt, porcelain, a bone-handled silver shovel and a single piece of mother-of-pearl.*

and the handles were decorated with bright-cut engraving or feather edging to give them extra sparkle.

In the 19th century all previous styles of spoon were reproduced, alongside new decorative patterns such as Albert, Coburg and Albany. Every type was made in silver and from the 1840s in electroplate. Some of the best companies marked their spoons with initials mimicking hallmarks – T B & S for Thomas Bradbury and Sons, E & Co for Elkingtons, and so on. Although electroplated spoons were usually made as cheaper alternatives, towards the end of the century some were designed as quality pieces. Elkingtons, for example, produced designs which incorporated champlevé, cloisonné and ivory.

VICTORIAN AND EDWARDIAN STYLES

Many spoons from the Georgian period, or even earlier, were 'improved' about 1880 with applied scallop-edged bowls and repoussé designs of fruit. These 'berry spoons' may also have had decoration added to the handle. Some consider this practice to have been Victorian vandalism, but the results are undeniably decorative, and berry spoons are now quite collectable.

The Edwardian period continued the Victorian taste, with a leavening of Art Nouveau with its characteristic flowing lines and decorations based on plants and other natural forms. Some of the best designs came from overseas, such as Georg Jensen's (from Denmark) and Christofle's (from France). In Britain Omar Ramsden, Alwyn Carr and C. R. Ashbee and the Guild of Handicrafts were the top designers of hand-made silver spoons. Ramsden and Carr revived figure knops and square steles wreathed in leaves and tendrils.

Not all art nouveau spoons were strictly functional: some had heart-shaped bowls and delicate openwork stems. The London store Liberty's was the biggest producer of machine-made Art Nouveau designs in silver and plate. The Cymric range, designed by Archibald Knox, took Celtic motifs as its inspiration. The range was sold elsewhere under different names and hallmarks (Liberty's had their own) but it is as Cymric that it is most collectable today. Liberty's sold Cymric until 1920, alongside a pewter version of the range known as Tudric.

SPECIALIST SPOONS

Spoons were generally all-purpose until the 18th century, when more specialized types began to appear associated with the growing habit of tea-drinking. Mote spoons had a perforated bowl for skimming floating leaves from tea and a pointed end for unclogging the spout. Teaspoons (and the almost identical coffee spoons) became highly decorated at the end of the century.

Even more extravagant decoration marked caddy spoons, which were introduced around 1770. These short-handled spoons had fanciful bowls in the shapes of such objects as shells, eagles' wings, jockey caps or leaves and were produced in large numbers in silver, plate and electroplate throughout the 19th century.

The Victorian love of gadgetry produced an

The caddy spoons shown here range in value from £42 for the 1899 silver spoon at bottom right to £300 for the 1815 leaf-shaped spoon with hoop handle, one of the most sought-after designs. The shell-shaped bowl or a shell motif on the handle are common features.

Hanoverian style, became known as Old English. The shape of the bowl also changed, becoming more oval, with the widest part near the handle. By mid-century, the basic modern shape had been firmly established.

Decoration became more and more elaborate as the century progressed. The underside of bowls were often die-struck with masonic, political or heraldic emblems. This was especially true of teaspoons; pictureback teaspoons from 1750-75 are sought-after today. Handle ends were scrolled and fluted

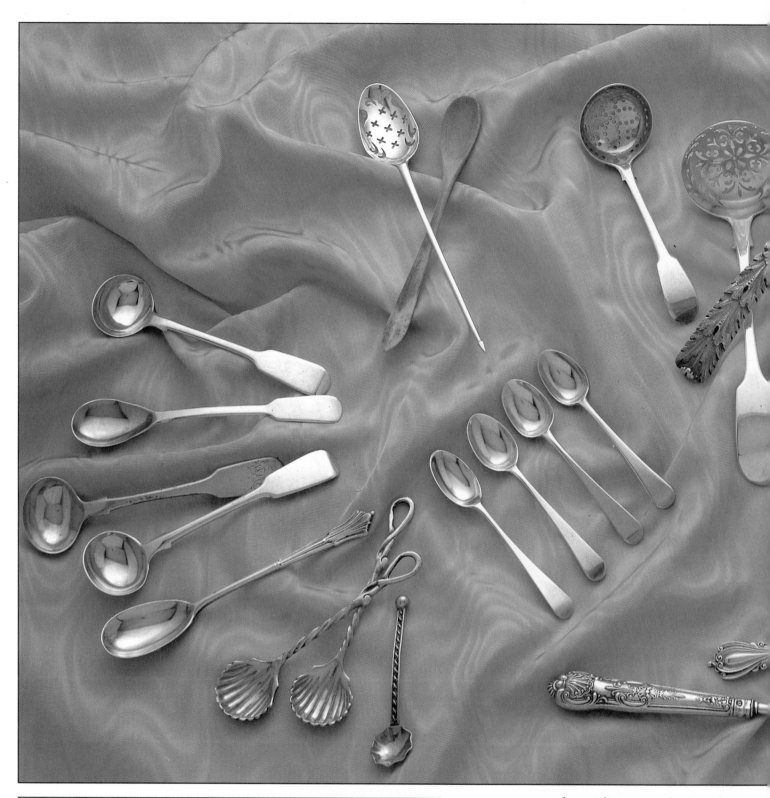

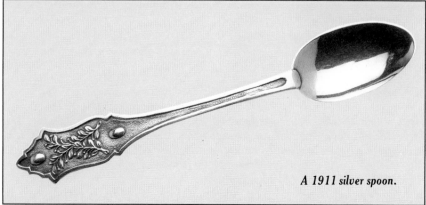

A 1911 silver spoon.

enormous range of specialist spoons for ice-cubes, ice-cream, ginger, olives, and so on. The flat-bowled, one-sided jam spoon was a late Victorian introduction, as was the round-bowled soup spoon. Souvenir spoons, usually teaspoons, marked with a town crest, reflected the Victorian and Edwardian love of travel.

Some spoons had gilded bowls to prevent tarnishing. Mid 18th-century salt spoons were shovel-shaped, with upturned handles, but after 1770 round bowls became more common. Mustard spoons, from the same era, have elliptical bowls and longer handles. Late 18th-century egg spoons have long bowls, while later examples have escutcheon

▲ *The all-silver spoon with a pierced handle is Edwardian. The other jam spoons are Victorian. Ivory handles (as here), or occasionally bone, were a popular feature. The spoon at the bottom with a vine pattern is of silver with a silver-gilt bowl.*

◄ *Clockwise from bottom left: 6 salt, 2 elliptical mustard, a pierced mote, a bone mustard, 4 sugar sifters, 3 bone egg, 2 sugar shovels and, centre, 4 snuff.*

BUILDING A COLLECTION

Most collectors specialize, collecting by firm, by city, by type or style of spoon, or by material — pewter, for example, is quite rare in old spoons as most were thrown away or broken, while silver was kept. Unusual materials include wood, bone, brass (before 1800) and ceramics. Spoons from the 18th century can still be found on market stalls, but earlier examples are the province of dealers and salesrooms. Examples from the 19th century, especially electroplated ones, are very easy to find, and very cheap; they offer the best field for those collecting for interest rather than investment or profit, especially from well-known firms such as Elkington, Mappin & Webb or Walker & Hall. Care should be taken to avoid any electroplated spoons that are worn or discoloured, as this lessens their value.

shapes. All-gold egg spoons with matching cups and a stand were produced around the middle of the Victorian period.

Love spoons, which were traditionally given as tokens of an engagement or a marriage, could be made in silver, wood or pewter, and depicted a couple embracing on their terminals. Wooden love spoons are a special case. Carved by prospective grooms from a single piece of wood, they often took the form of two spoons linked by a chain, with pierced motifs.

Most wooden love spoons are Welsh, from the late 17th to the 19th century, but French, German and Norwegian examples can also be found.

·PRICE GUIDE· SPOONS

Early apostle spoons are priced at around £300 and up, depending on date. A good quality trefid spoon will be about £300, while an 18th-century Hanoverian or Old English will be around £50-80. Genuine pictureback teaspoons are around the same price. A 19th-century silver spoon will be in the £5-10 range, though early examples may be much more, while electroplated spoons should cost between £1 and £5. Regency caddy spoons can be very expensive. The most sought-after are jockey caps, at around £200, and eagle's wings, at around £600. Other designs range from £40 to £150. Single art nouveau spoons by named makers are £100 and up. As a general rule, a set of six spoons will cost ten times as much as a single example.

Sugar Tongs
and
Sugar Nips

To the Georgians, tea was an expensive luxury, served with
due ceremony and with a variety of silver
accoutrements by a hostess

The Georgian period, which marked the rapid expansion of the British Empire, also witnessed an extraordinary increase in the English partiality for what one detractor described as 'the tea menace'. Soon every self-respecting 18th-century hostess was obliged to dazzle her guests with an armoury of accoutrements – tea caddies, teapots, strainer or 'mote' spoons, sugar baskets, milk jugs, creamers, teaspoons, caddy spoons, tea kettles and sugar tongs or nips – most of which were fashioned from silver.

Tea, that 'Sov'reign Drink of Pleasure and of Health' as one 18th-century poet described it, first arrived in England for sale to the general public in 1657. By 1718, the beginning of the Georgian era, tea had taken over from silk as the East India Company's most important trading article. Thirty years later Dr Johnson was roundly declaring himself 'a hardened and shameless tea-drinker' (he frequently drank at least ten cups at a sitting), and the provision of tea 'twice-daily' had become a condition of employment. Tea was here to stay.

The new beverage was by no means cheap, costing the equivalent of between £80 and £100 in today's currency per pound. Increasingly heavy taxation in the form of excise duty on luxury goods encouraged widespread smuggling. Those who could afford tea treated it with great respect. Caddies, equipped with their own lock and key, were kept in the drawing room.

TIME FOR TEA

Four o'clock tea was an invention of the Victorian period. The Georgians took tea at different times of day, the lady of the house perhaps refreshing herself in the drawing room after the tedium of the morning toilette with a cup, or pouring tea for her lady friends. Tea could also be taken in the popular coffee houses or pleasure gardens of the day. After dinner, which usually began at 4pm, the ladies would leave the dining room to brew and drink tea and coffee in the drawing room until they were joined by the gentlemen around 7pm.

Ritual played its part. A guest would intimate that her cup was empty by balancing a spoon across the top, by using it to tap the cup, or by turning the cup upside down on to the saucer, so that her male escort or a servant could remove it.

Leaves of Bohea, Congou or Souchong (black tea varieties) and Singlo or Hyson (green tea) would be taken from the caddy or caddies with the caddy spoon and mixed by the hostess. Water was added to the small teapot from the tea kettle which was usually equipped with a spirit lamp and stand to keep the water hot. Stray tea leaves floating on the top of the brew would be skimmed off with the 'mote' spoon, the pointed end of which was used to clear blockages in the teapot's spout.

The addition of milk and sugar became increasingly popular. The latter, imported in large sugar 'loaves', was not consumed in the quantities it is today, though by the end of the 18th century per capita intake had risen by 750 per cent. Steel 'nips' were an essential kitchen utensil designed to prize pieces from the loaf.

Silver became the preferred metal for teaware from teapot to sugar tongs, though Sheffield Plate was also used in the late Georgian era. The low cost of silversmithing relative to the cost of the metal per ounce meant that work could be commissioned as an investment. The market was still being flooded with

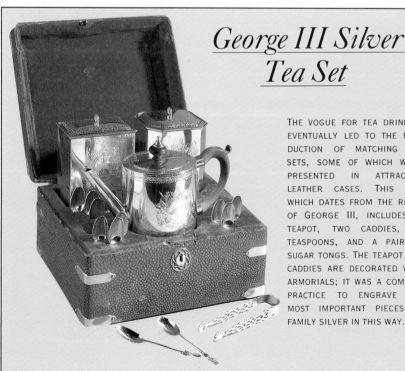

George III Silver
Tea Set

THE VOGUE FOR TEA DRINKING EVENTUALLY LED TO THE PRO-DUCTION OF MATCHING TEA SETS, SOME OF WHICH WERE PRESENTED IN ATTRACTIVE LEATHER CASES. THIS SET, WHICH DATES FROM THE REIGN OF GEORGE III, INCLUDES A TEAPOT, TWO CADDIES, 12 TEASPOONS, AND A PAIR OF SUGAR TONGS. THE TEAPOT AND CADDIES ARE DECORATED WITH ARMORIALS; IT WAS A COMMON PRACTICE TO ENGRAVE THE MOST IMPORTANT PIECES OF FAMILY SILVER IN THIS WAY.

▲ *This painting from the early 18th century shows an English family indulging in the newly fashionable habit of taking tea. They are drinking from elegant cups without handles, and on the table in front of them are spread several attractive silver accessories – a tea kettle and stand, a slop bowl, a tall jug, a tea caddy, a sugar bowl, teaspoons and a pair of sugar tongs.*

silver from the New World and at the same time England was benefiting from changes in manufacturing techniques and the arrival of highly skilled Huguenot silversmiths, who had been forced to flee France as a result of persecution under Louis XIV.

THE SUGAR TONGS

The evolution of sugar tongs or nips from the late 17th century through to the end of the Georgian era is a reflection in miniature of the changing styles and techniques that characterize the period. The earliest examples, from the last quarter of the 17th century and the early decades of the 18th, resemble blacksmith's or fireside tongs and are rarely found today, except in museums.

Cast in two pieces, the long, slender arms of these early tongs were joined by repeated heating and hammering to provide the necessary tensile spring. This part was often surmounted by a finial, while the ends terminated in a shallow spade shape. Ornamentation was simple, imitating the baluster or spiral design used in andiron decoration.

Later models were made from a continuous piece of silver wire, controlled by arc-shaped oval grips. The bowls were initially a flat oval shape, but by

Nips and Tongs

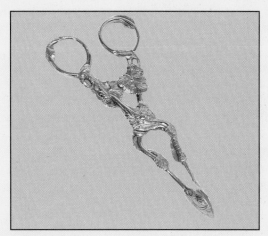

A HIGHLY ELABORATE PAIR OF SCISSOR-ACTION SUGAR NIPS IN SILVER GILT, WITH LEAF DECORATION. THEY WERE MADE AROUND 1715 BY GEORGE GILLINGHAM.

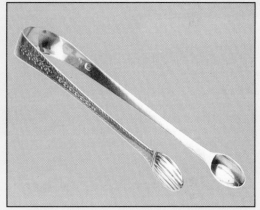

A PAIR OF SILVER TONGS MADE BY GEORGE SMITH IN 1785. WITH THEIR RESTRAINED DECORATION AND SIMPLE LINES THEY ANTICIPATE MANY MODERN DESIGNS.

THESE CURIOUS SUGAR NIPS IN THE FORM OF SERPENTS ENTWINED WITH BRANCHES WERE MADE BY SAMUEL HENNELL IN 1815. THE ENDS ARE FORMED FROM THE SERPENTS' HEADS.

Glass and Metalware

1730 these had become curved, sporting die-stamped ornamentation or rat-tail joins to match contemporary spoons. Occasionally, a central spike used to clear the teapot spout was included. These early tongs were rarely fully hallmarked.

The end of the 17th century had already seen the advent of the metal rolling mill. The man-hours required to hammer out ingots were thus drastically reduced and silver sheeting became much lighter in weight and therefore less costly. This is reflected in the increasing number of tongs manufactured as the 18th century progressed and hence in their relative cheapness for the collector.

THE SUGAR NIPS

By the 1730s the influence of the French 'rocaille' decoration with its emphasis on sea and rock themes (which included mythical monsters, sea gods and crustacea), sponsored by great Huguenot silver-smiths such as Paul de Lamerie, was beginning to make itself felt. The scissor-type of sugar nips, initially appearing around 1715, were the first to be decorated in the new fashion.

The bowls were frequently cast in the shape of scallop shells, the shanks elaborately scrolled and the large, box-like central pivot engraved, often with the

·PRICE GUIDE·⟩ SILVER TEA ACCESSORIES

Silver tea accessories are among the most attractive collectables from the Georgian period. Matching sets of caddies and teapots with fine decoration tend to be expensive, but smaller items such as nips and tongs are most affordable.

▲ *A charming illustration of the ceremony of tea drinking in the mid-Georgian era. The lady at the tea table lifts a sugar lump from the bowl with a pair of tongs; her graceful china cups appear to be imports from the Far East. On the left, a man is about to place a tea kettle on a stand.*

▶ *A silver sugar basket with attractive pierced decoration, and a hallmark indicating that it was made in London in 1769.*

PRICE GUIDE **5**

▲ *A pair of George III sugar nips with scallop shell grips, and the owner's initials engraved on the hinge box.*

▲ *A pair of George II silver sugar nips from c.1750. They carry the maker's initials H.P.*

▲ *An early pair of sugar nips dating from around 1720, made by William Atkinson.*

PRICE GUIDE **5**

PRICE GUIDE **5**

PRICE GUIDE **6**

owner's crest or initials. Sugar nips were usually quite small, measuring not more than 17 inches (42cm) in length. Maker's marks and hallmarks on sugar nips in early rococo pieces can be located inside the nips; later examples were stamped inside the finger grips, but it is rare in either case for these marks to be complete.

Decoration became increasingly elaborate, with the result that silverware became almost totally covered with florid ornament in high relief. Sugar nips of this type were cast and rarely hallmarked, with the result that they were much reproduced in the Victorian period. These later reproductions lack the finesse of their originals.

Novelty Georgian sugar nips are extremely rare. The stork type is perhaps the best known but the collector must again beware of Victorian imitations.

Sugar nips were often manufactured with matching spoons. Occasionally they formed part of a canteen which included caddies, spoons, knives and a mote spoon. It was not until the 1770s that the tea service as we know it today came into being.

Tongs reappeared in the 1770s in the U-shape familiar to the tea-drinkers of today. Their similarity to spoons meant they could be more closely matched, utilizing shapes such as the fiddle pattern and thread and shell pattern decoration, which echoed the more restrained style of the Adam period.

These tongs were either cast with the 'U' section well hammered to ensure sufficient elasticity, or made from a continuous piece of flattened silver wire to create the so-called 'bow tongs'. The cast variety are usually more decorated, the bowl section with scallop shells or acanthus leaves, for example, and the arms with floral or plant patterns or even tiny human figures. As a result, these tend to fetch a little more than double the price of the 'bow' variety. Both types favour the openwork style ornamentation. Towards the end of the century mother-of-pearl was occasionally used for the shank section.

Birmingham and Sheffield plate were used increasingly from the 1760s on. Harder steel gouging tools led to the use of a 'fly press' for accurate and repetitive piercing and a new engraving technique called bright cutting. Pretty faceted decoration was much used for tea services and individual pieces including tea spoons, sugar tongs and caddy spoons. It was particularly favoured in the Regency period being used on the tong shanks and on the bowls.

Collecting sugar tongs and nips can be an inexpensive and rewarding hobby. However, the prospective buyer must beware of later imitations.

◀▶ *A set of two tea caddies and a sugar bowl with a cover, all with matching heavily embossed decoration of flowers, leaves and scrolls. The set was made in 1758 by Samuel Taylor.*

PRICE GUIDE **8**

▼ *These rather short and squat sugar tongs are simple and functional. They date from 1814.*

PRICE GUIDE **2**

▲ *A very plain pair of silver tongs dating from 1808. The maker is not known.*

PRICE GUIDE **2**

▲ *Late Regency sugar tongs from 1822, with bowls that resemble those found on spoons of the period.*

PRICE GUIDE **2**

Silver Tableware

In the modestly furnished dining rooms of Georgian England,
the beautifully crafted silver that glittered upon the table was
the most obvious sign of a family's wealth

During the late 17th and early 18th centuries English silver underwent several changes in design and workmanship. The quantity and range of items produced also increased to meet the demand created by a newly prosperous middle class. The silver trade itself was injected with new vigour from the large numbers of Protestant Huguenot craftsmen and their families who fled from persecution in France to England following the revocation of the Edict of Nantes in 1685, bringing with them new ideas and skills. At first rejected by native goldsmiths, they were eventually assimilated until, in the second generation, some rose to the very height of their calling: the celebrated silversmith Paul de Lamerie was of Huguenot descent.

FRENCH INFLUENCE

The French influence on English silver at this time was very marked: silversmiths began to use a thicker gauge of metal for all but the very cheapest wares, or those intended for humble domestic use such as the two-handled porringers (fluted to give greater strength), which were popular until almost the middle of the 18th century. Designs became more sophisticated, at first following the taste for heavy ornament popular at the French Court, and then, in the mid-1730s, adopting the lighter but still elaborate rococo style.

Well-mannered asymmetrical patterns of scrolls and flowers were selected by silver chasers to decorate the surfaces of already well-established shapes in the silversmiths' repertoire, from snuff boxes to soup tureens. The Parisian predeliction for extreme rococo forms, in which rocks and shells, sea foam and weeds engulfed the whole piece, was almost totally ignored in England.

The rococo style of decoration gave way in the 1760s to neo-classical forms. The architects Robert and James Adam worked

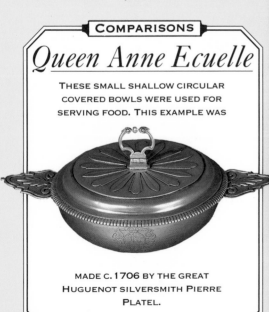

in this idiom, producing a number of exclusive designs for silver inspired by studies of ancient Roman remains. Surviving items in the precious metal known to have been based on their work are very opulent, and were obviously expensive and time-consuming to produce.

Although the silver and allied trades were greatly influenced for the next quarter of a century by the style, few adopted the Adams' full-blown neo-classical vocabulary; for the general run of wares it was simply not commercially viable. On the other hand, the ever expanding market constantly challenged silversmiths with its demands for wares of different qualities. The wealthy landowner might order his

▲ Sparkling silver and glass add a touch of glamour to this lovely dining room. The individual pieces of silver are far from ostentatious; their restrained classicism blends in perfectly with the understated elegance of the room.

◀ Tureens, sauce boats, platters and condiment sets in silver or Sheffield plate will always look impressive as part of a sideboard buffet presentation, but collectors of modest means may have to confine themselves to the smaller pieces such as salt, pepper or mustard pots.

expensive and stylish dinner service from the King's own goldsmith, Thomas Heming in Bond Street, just as the shopkeeper could buy cheaply-produced, modestly-priced candlesticks from Thomas Daniell's London Silver Plate Manufactory in the City.

Many such candlesticks were mass-produced in Sheffield, a relatively new manufacturing town for silver and plated goods. Like Birmingham, it won the right in 1773 to open its own assay office. Previously, silversmiths in both towns had been obliged to send goods to London (probably in an unfinished state) for hallmarking, a costly exercise which annoyed businessmen whose ambitions were always to expand into new markets at home and abroad. The success of a manufacturer such as Matthew Boulton depended upon an efficient use of materials and local manpower, and these were qualities for which his Soho factory, which was built near Birmingham at about

1764, was famous all over the civilised world.

A thoroughly up-to-date version of the die-stamp, which was capable of producing many copies of the same embossed decoration upon metal, had been employed at Birmingham in the snuff box and button business since the mid-1740s. Inevitably, some of the London silversmiths with old-fashioned methods objected to such techniques and to manufacturers like Boulton whose workforce was encouraged to use them. But Londoners had to live with the fact that mass-production had come to stay. Some, such as the candlestick maker John Carter, even ordered cheap die-stamped items from Sheffield and had them marked in London as if they were his own.

CAST WORK

Of course, high quality cast work, for those to whom cost was of little concern, continued to be made, but some London manufacturers saw great potential in the new methods. Improved machinery, developed in the Sheffield plate trade where thin sheet metal of a uniform standard was essential, was soon employed in some of the London workshops. Hester Bateman, a middle-aged widow with a couple of energetic sons and their wives as business assistants, ran the busiest of London's silver factories in the 1770s. All manner of middle-range work, much fashioned from the new sheet and with applied machine-milled beaded wire borders, poured from their premises in Bunhill Row.

Solid Silver Tableware

Although Georgian dining rooms were usually modestly furnished, there was ample opportunity for displaying wealth at the dining table. The silver épergne, a sprawling centrepiece for fruit and other delicacies, was a French invention adopted with enthusiasm in England. Around it were placed salt cellars, sometimes with blue glass liners, mustard pots, and other vessels for every other kind of ketchup and condiment. The more expensive were either of silver or of glass with silver mounts.

Candles in candlesticks illu-minated the scene, their light reflected in the silver and glass on the table. Wine bottles or glass decanters stood in silver coasters and the meal was con-sumed with silver spoons and forks or with silver-handled steel knives from Sheffield. Silver plates and serving dishes were a luxury, as were the many gadgets which made their appearance after the 1760s: dish rings and the adjustable dish crosses (with burners) for supporting hot plates; and ingenious little wedges to tip meat dishes for easy access to the gravy.

▲ *A silver plate with a gadrooned rim, made by Smith and Sharp in 1787. It is one of 12 identical plates, and the price guide is for the set.*

PRICE GUIDE **9**

▲ *Silver egg boiler, stand and heater made by Emes and Bernard in 1809. The boiler holds four eggs and incorporates a useful timer.*

PRICE GUIDE **9**

▲▶ *A pair of early George III silver wine coasters, with vertical sides pierced with scroll and leaf motifs, made by Thomas Nash of London.*

PRICE GUIDE **8**

▶ *Silver salt cellar with pierced decoration and a blue glass lining, made by Thomas Shepherd in 1790. It is one of a set of four salt cellars, and the price guide is for the complete set.*

PRICE GUIDE **7**

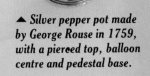

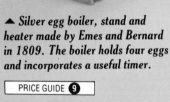

▲ *Silver pepper pot made by George Rouse in 1759, with a pierced top, balloon centre and pedestal base.*

PRICE GUIDE **7**

▲ *Silver trumpet-shaped funnel for decanting wine, made in 1828 by Emes and Bernard.*

PRICE GUIDE **7**

▲ Silver soup tureen designed by Thomas Whipham in 1748. It has splayed feet, decorative reeded borders, and ornate handles.

PRICE GUIDE **9**

▲ One of a pair of wood and silver coasters dating from the reign of George III and made by William Elliott. They are large enough to hold a magnum. The price guide is for the pair.

PRICE GUIDE **8**

▲ Silver toast rack from 1818, made by William Sharp. It has a gadrooned border, lion's-paw feet, and a handle with leaf and scroll moulding.

PRICE GUIDE **7**

◀ Silver mustard pot made by Robert Hennell in 1789. The oval-shaped body has pierced decoration, and there is a ball finial on the lid.

PRICE GUIDE **7**

◀ Silver salt cellar from 1814 made by S. C. Younge. It has a silver gilt interior, three lion's-paw legs, and gadrooned and scalloped borders.

PRICE GUIDE **6**

PRICE GUIDE

Sheffield Plate Tableware

The Sheffield plate industry was established after 1743, when it was discovered by a lucky chance that a sheet of silver and another of copper, when fused together by heat, could be worked as a single metal. It was not until the 1760s, however, that improved techniques allowed manufacturers to make anything larger than buttons and snuff boxes. Once perfected, the new material was admirably suited to the production of hollow articles such as tankards, sauce tureens and coffee pots, or items such as candlesticks and salvers which, if carefully handled, would retain their covering of silver for many years.

Among the most impressive items to have survived from the 18th century in Sheffield plate are tea urns and bread baskets, the latter often pierced with complicated patterns like their counterparts in solid silver. Candlesticks, too, were made from stamped parts, each section being struck separately before being assembled by hand and filled with pitch for stability.

▲ An elegant Sheffield plate soup tureen from 1795. Decoration is minimal since the design depends on simplicity for its impact, but there are fish motif handles and gadrooned borders.

PRICE GUIDE **8**

▼ An unmarked two bottle decanter wagon dating from c.1820. The coasters have convex spiral flutes and bold gadroon shell and acanthus mounts applied to their top surfaces.

PRICE GUIDE **7**

▲ One of a pair, this Sheffield plate oval sauce boat has a beaded rim, a double scrolling beaded handle, and three hoof and bold leaf feet. The price guide is for the pair.

PRICE GUIDE **7**

◀ *Epergne c.1825, consisting of cut glass dishes supported by a heavily ornamented Sheffield plate stand.*

PRICE GUIDE **8**

▼ *One from a set of four sweetmeat dishes made in 1795 by Pitts and Preedy. Cut glass dishes sit on stands with elegant leaf motifs and splayed feet. The price guide is for the set.*

PRICE GUIDE **9**

▲ *One of a set of four neo-classical candlesticks from 1775. The base is decorated with dolphins, and a vine winds its way round the stem of the column. The price is for the whole set.*

PRICE GUIDE **8**

▼◀ *Unmarked two-handled Sheffield plate tray from c.1770. There is an engraved crest in the centre, and the edge is chased with a slanting gadroon border. There are rope-like handles.*

PRICE GUIDE **5**

PRICE GUIDE

COLLECTOR'S TIPS

The best advice a new collector can take is to buy what he or she likes. It is not worth buying with the intention of making a quick profit: even in the field of English silver, where the hallmark gives a false sense of security, there are several potential pitfalls to be avoided.

Unfortunately, much of the silver which would have been found in the 18th-century dining room is now very expensive; those without ample resources cannot seriously think of purchasing a soup tureen or an épergne. Even only moderately good examples will run to several thousand pounds. The choice, however, is better among the smaller items such as casters and wine coasters, mustard pots and salt cellars, although caution is essential. Salt cellars, especially, must be selected with care and knowledge. These items were produced throughout the 18th century, in different qualities ranging from the magnificent to the cheap and nasty. One of the worst mistakes a collector can make is to think that because an object is old it must be good. The Hennell family of manufacturing silversmiths, who had a substantial corner of the salt cellar market for 80 years, produced only average wares and these, when worn, may not be worth buying. There is nothing more depressing than finding one of their compressed circular salts, of which they produced thousands in the 1740s and 1750s, which has been so well used that the marks have all but disappeared!

LATER FAKES

Collectors should know that there are still many fakes of English silver at large. A few spectacular examples are of relatively modern origin, but the bulk are of ordinary wares and were probably made between

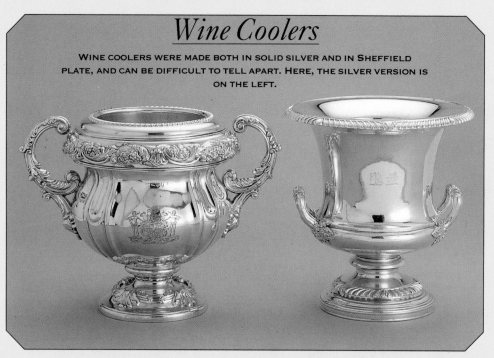

Wine Coolers

WINE COOLERS WERE MADE BOTH IN SOLID SILVER AND IN SHEFFIELD PLATE, AND CAN BE DIFFICULT TO TELL APART. HERE, THE SILVER VERSION IS ON THE LEFT.

George III Silver Epergne

EPERGNES — CENTREPIECES WITH SEVERAL BOWLS OR BASKETS FOR FRUIT, NUTS AND SWEETMEATS — REACHED HEIGHTS OF ELABORATION DURING THE GEORGIAN PERIOD. THIS SPLENDID EXAMPLE — CLEARLY INFLUENCED BY THE ROCOCO STYLE — WAS MADE BY WILLIAM TUITE OF LONDON IN 1770. IT HAS AN UNDULATING CENTRE WHICH FLARES OUTWARD AT THE BASE, WITH PIERCED AND CAST FLORAL DECORATION. THE OVAL CENTRE BASKET HAS A FLARED WAVY RIM DECORATED WITH GADROON, SHELL AND SCROLL MOTIFS. FOUR DOUBLE SCROLLING LEGS END IN TRIANGULAR FEET, AND FOUR ARMS SUPPORT SHALLOW DISHES.

① MOST PARTS OF THE ÉPERGNE ARE DETACHABLE; THE CENTRAL DISH LIFTS OUT OF ITS NICHE, AS DO THE SIDE DISHES, AND THE SUPPORTING ARMS UNSCREW.

② THE FLAT DISHES ARE CHASED WITH FORMAL SCROLL MOTIFS.

③ THE CENTRAL DECORATION IS BOTH PIERCED AND CAST.

④ THE TRIANGULAR FEET HAVE CAST LEAFY DECORATION.

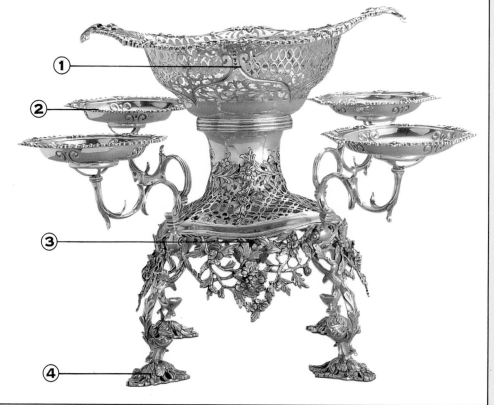

·CLOSE UP·

① SHELL MOTIFS

③ PIERCED DECORATION AND BEADING

⑤ HALLMARK AND MAKER'S MARK

② WORN SHEFFIELD PLATE

④ ARMORIAL CREST

⑥ LION'S-HEAD HANDLE

① SHELL MOTIFS ARE A STANDARD FORM OF DECORATION ON GEORGIAN SILVER.

② THE COPPER CORE OFTEN SHOWS THROUGH THE SILVER COATING ON SHEFFIELD PLATE.

③ PIERCING AND BEADING ARE FREQUENTLY SEEN ON GEORGIAN DOMESTIC SILVER.

④ FAMILY CRESTS WERE OFTEN ENGRAVED ON PRIZED SILVER HEIRLOOMS.

⑤ THE HALLMARK SHOWS THE MUSTARD POT TO HAVE BEEN MADE BY ROBERT HENNELL IN 1787.

⑥ LION'S HEADS AND PAWS WERE FAVOURITE MOTIFS WITH GEORGIAN SILVERSMITHS.

about 1875 and 1940. If at all unsure, obtain advice from an independent expert; if necessary, there are provisions in law to protect you against an unlucky purchase from an unrepentant dealer.

Fakes tend to fall into two categories. The first comprises items which bear genuine marks lifted from the object upon which they were originally struck. Typically, one may find marks from a spoon let into the foot of a cup. The second is where the marks as well as the object are spurious. At the close of the 19th century, a London silversmith called Charles Twinham received a five year prison sentence for making many such items in his garden shed. Other types of silver to be wary of are 'duty dodgers'. These are items where the maker has used an old hallmarked piece of silver in order to avoid paying the duty. It was a practice in which several early 18th-century silversmiths indulged.

ALTERATIONS AND ADDITIONS

Beware, furthermore, of the altered item. Any unmarked addition to a piece of hallmarked English silver – for instance, adding a spout to a tankard to transform it into a jug – is deemed illegal and the item cannot therefore be offered for sale in the United Kingdom. Articles with later chased decoration, while not usually recom-mended for the inexperienced collector, are not classed as fakes.

Silver in daily use may be kept clean by washing in warm soapy water and then rinsing and drying immediately. Drips will leave a temporary stain.

Do not cover the marks with sticky tape in the belief that it will preserve them; it will not, because the adhesive contains a substance that will actually attack the surface of the silver as surely as if one tied a set of teaspoons together with a rubber band.

Never rub silver with abrasives to remove salt stains. Such repairs can only be effected by an experienced silversmith. The latter are a dwindling breed, so be very careful to whom you entrust even the most humble item in your collection.

Some collectors, rather than clean their silver, will have items lacquered, or plated with non-tarnishing rhodium. The first is not advisable because the lacquer 'deadens' the surface and will discolour in time. The second is an irreversible process, so you must be sure you prefer your silver looking like chrome before having it done!

POINTS TO WATCH
■ Look for signs of soldering around the feet of tureens and sauce boats, and for seaming under handles; these are weak points which may have undergone repair.

■ Make sure that hallmarks and dates are identical on pairs or sets of pieces, and on the base and cover of items such as casters and dredgers.

■ Crests or initials engraved at a later date detract from value, as does their removal (signalled by a thinner area of silver).

■ Electroplate imitations of Sheffield plate are very difficult to distinguish from the genuine item, particularly if copper has been used as the core. Seek expert advice before buying.

▲ *Two George II candlesticks in the rococo style, made by John Edwards of London.*

Edwardian Table Silver

The beautifully polished knives, forks and spoons that sparkled
on the Edwardian dining table delighted the hostess and her
guests with their dignified, traditional designs

No Edwardian dining room, whether in some aristocratic mansion or in a modest suburban villa, would have been complete without its canteen of table silver. In fact, canteens had become important in all respectable households long before 1901 when Edward VII ascended the throne, and they were as essential to the efficient hostess as the linen tablecloths and napkins, the silver or electroplated entrée dishes and the porcelain dinner plates with which her table was laden.

Edwardian silversmiths were able to supply canteens in several different styles and finishes to suit all pockets. From the traditional plain Old English, a pattern which had evolved during the 18th century, to richly decorated and sometimes gilt items suitable only for fruit and puddings, the choice was vast.

THE ENGLISH CANTEEN

Nevertheless, unlike most sets of table silver manufactured abroad – in France, Germany and North America, for instance – the English canteen was a relatively simple affair often consisting of just two sizes of knives, spoons and forks for the main and dessert courses, tea or coffee spoons and several implements for serving soup or vegetables and, perhaps, a pair of carvers. To these could be added soup spoons (invented in the 1880s), fish knives and

▶ *Edwardian table silver can add distinction to the sideboard and table of a modern home. Smaller sets, such as those containing fish knives and forks, butter knives or coffee spoons, are generally easier to find and cheaper than large canteens with several place settings and serving implements.*

Travelling Canteen

MADE IN AUGSBURG IN 1730, THIS TRAVELLING CANTEEN
FITS NEATLY INTO A LEATHER CASE. IT CONTAINS SILVER GILT
FLATWARE AND CUTLERY FOR A SINGLE PLACE SETTING, AND
AN EGG CUP AND BOWL.

forks (rarely found before the 1860s, although some of 1828 have been recorded), fish slices, butter knives and salt and egg spoons.

Individual items of flatware were traditionally made by specialist workshops. Silver spoon makers had been established in Britain since Roman times, and several 19th-century concerns whose names – Chawner & Co., Holland, Aldwinckle &

▲ *The tables in fashionable Edwardian hotels exuded an air of opulence with their sparkling displays of silver and glass.*

Slater and Francis Higgins & Son – are familiar to all serious collectors of Victorian and Edwardian table silver, were able, by virtue of successions of apprenticeship, to trace connections with their counterparts who had flourished under Elizabeth I.

Forks are believed to have been introduced to Europe by the Italians, and they were probably added to the London silver spoon makers' repertoire during the 16th century. The earliest English silver fork to have survived, now in the Victoria and Albert Museum, dates from 1632. By contrast, in this country the manufacture of cutlery – edged steel goods such as knives and razors – is of ancient origin and is a branch of the business quite distinct from that of the silver spoon and fork maker. In the case of knives, it is only when the blades are finished that the silversmith is required to supply and fix the handles. Over the past three centuries or so English cutlers have traditionally worked in London and in Sheffield.

EDWARDIAN REVIVALISM
There were very few innovations in English table silver design during the late Victorian and Edwardian periods. It was an age fascinated by the luxuries of the 18th and early 19th centuries – a fact amply demonstrated by furniture and ladies' fashions – and much tableware was designed in direct imitation of earlier styles.

Most well-known 18th-century patterns in spoons and forks were available, from the robust Hanoverian Rat-tail to the more

delicate Old English which could be supplied either plain or with 'feathered' edges. It seems likely that at the turn of the century the sales of these two designs outstripped most others, with the possible exception of King's – an ornate pattern, of which there were many variants, which had first become popular around 1810. Such richly adorned pieces were more difficult to manufacture than the plain versions, but advances made over the next 100 years equipped the table silver trade for semi mass-production.

BLANKS AND DIES
In the making of spoons and forks, 'blanks' were prepared from flattened strips of silver (or nickel if the items were to be electroplated). These were then cut roughly to shape before being put into the steel die. In one version of the technique, the die was made in the form of a 'box' and 'lid', each section of which was engraved with the pattern in reverse. Once the blank was inside the box die, the whole was pressed between powerful rollers, after which the blank emerged as a recognizable but unfinished spoon or fork complete with its design. The following stages, all accomplished by hand, took the patterned blank from the trimmer via the silversmith (who imparted the distinctive shape) to the buffer for final polishing. Even though the process is labour intensive and requires great skill, the industry is still carried on in much the same way today.

In England immediately before World War I, table silver was mainly made in specialized workshops in London, Birmingham and Sheffield. The only exceptions were the manufacturing silversmiths, Josiah Williams & Co. of Bristol, who were put out of business by enemy action in 1940.

Knives, Forks and Spoons

When laid for dinner, the principal items on the Edwardian dining table would have been arranged in much the same way as they are today, although there might have been one or two decorative flourishes, such as a silver bowl of roses in the centre. Traditional hostesses, however, shunning the soup spoon as an unattractive modern 'refinement', would have preferred the old-fashioned tablespoon for the soup course.

Besides the usual knives, spoons and forks, and depending upon the menu, other implements might be laid, including lobster picks and individual butter knives. In Edwardian times the choice was almost limitless and, as one contemporary advertisement put it, 'Canteens can be fitted to hold any quantity of Spoons and Forks, and if desired, Cutlery also.'

The patterns most readily available were Old English and its variants such as Beaded and Shell, Fiddle and Rat-tail. These had all been popular for many decades, as had the ostentatious King's.

Other rich patterns, including Albany and Prince's could be purchased without much trouble. But Edwardian silversmiths were also able to supply to special order many older patterns. Among these were Grecian, Palm, Threaded Shell and, similar to King's, the slightly more refined Queen's.

▶ *Knife, fork and spoon in the Feather Edge style – a variation on the Old English pattern.*

PRICE GUIDE **4**

▼ *Edwardian silver knife, with a pistol handle, in the Onslow pattern.*

PRICE GUIDE **3**

▲ *Edwardian Albany silver fork and spoon in the Onslow pattern, with typical fluted handles.*

PRICE GUIDE **4**

▲ *Silver pastry fork, dessert knife and soup spoons – all Victorian inventions – in the Grecian style.*

PRICE GUIDE **4**

▼ *Fish knife, fish fork and coffee spoon in the elegant La Regence pattern.*

PRICE GUIDE **4**

▲ *Edwardian silver Beaded pattern knife, fork and spoon.*

PRICE GUIDE **4**

PRICE GUIDE

▼ *A knife and spoon in the Du Barry pattern are paired with a fork in the Jesmond style.*

PRICE GUIDE ❹

▲ *Knife, with a stainless steel blade, and spoon in the Jesmond pattern, by Thomas Ward of Sheffield.*

PRICE GUIDE ❹

▼ *Edwardian Fiddle Thread knife and fork. The design dates from the early 19th century.*

PRICE GUIDE ❹

▼ *Silver knife, fork and spoon in the Hanoverian pattern – popular since the 18th century.*

PRICE GUIDE ❹

▼ *A silver Old English monogrammed fork and spoon flank an Old English knife.*

PRICE GUIDE ❹

▲ *Elaborately decorated silver knife, fork and spoon in the Venetian pattern.*

PRICE GUIDE ❹

PRICE GUIDE

Serving Items

In English canteens there were usually none of the ice cream and sorbet spoons, cake servers, sugar sifters and the dozens of other 'necessities' which were found in continental and in North American sets. Here, this class of goods was sold separately, reposing in their satin and velvet-lined boxes covered in morocco leather (or in embossed black paper if a cheaper article was required).

They were marketed as wedding gifts or as presents for Christmas and other special occasions, and were not necessarily expensive: a registered design 'Jam-Spoon, Pickle-Fork, and Butter-Knife, in case,' could be bought from Mappin & Webb in silver for two guineas and in electroplate for just 15 shillings.

Fish servers, already popular in Victorian times, were now made in hundreds of different finishes. They sometimes had gilt or engraved blades, and the handles were often of ivory or mother-of-pearl. Meat and poultry carving sets, some with silver-mounted stag or buck horn handles, made ideal gifts for gentlemen. Serving spoons for salad were popular as were large spoons for stewed fruit, and the design for such items became very fanciful.

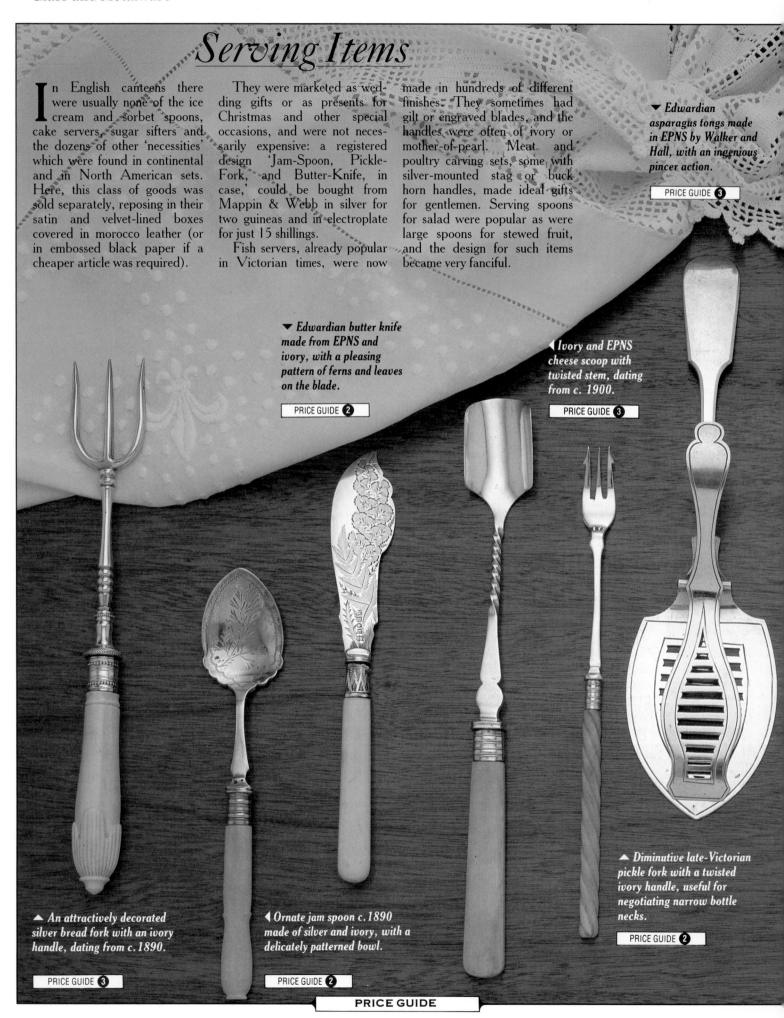

▼ *Edwardian asparagus tongs made in EPNS by Walker and Hall, with an ingenious pincer action.*

PRICE GUIDE ③

▼ *Edwardian butter knife made from EPNS and ivory, with a pleasing pattern of ferns and leaves on the blade.*

PRICE GUIDE ②

◀ *Ivory and EPNS cheese scoop with twisted stem, dating from c. 1900.*

PRICE GUIDE ③

▲ *An attractively decorated silver bread fork with an ivory handle, dating from c. 1890.*

PRICE GUIDE ③

◀ *Ornate jam spoon c. 1890 made of silver and ivory, with a delicately patterned bowl.*

PRICE GUIDE ②

▲ *Diminutive late-Victorian pickle fork with a twisted ivory handle, useful for negotiating narrow bottle necks.*

PRICE GUIDE ②

PRICE GUIDE

◀ A turn-of-the-century EPNS lobster pick used for extracting the meat from awkward corners of the shell. It is decorated with an engraved lobster.

PRICE GUIDE ❶

◀ Edwardian soup ladle in the Beaded pattern, made in EPNS.

PRICE GUIDE ❷

◀ A carving knife and fork in EPNS with steel blade and prongs. The monogram suggests that they were once part of a complete canteen.

PRICE GUIDE ❹

▲ Matching fish knife and fork in EPNS, showing some discoloration.

PRICE GUIDE ❸

PRICE GUIDE

COLLECTOR'S TIPS

Collectors of Victorian and Edwardian table silver are in the fortunate position of having a mass of material from which to choose. Before World War II, the workshops which specialized in such wares were producing an astonishing range in vast quantities for sale both at home and abroad. The fact that the export market was so large was partly due to the extent of the Empire and partly because English-made table silver was traditionally recognized as the finest in the world.

Although English table silver is somewhat conservative in design – the Americans were much more adventurous – the spoons and forks made in Chawner & Co.'s or Francis Higgins & Son's long-defunct London factories are extremely comfortable to eat with. The proprietors and senior craftsmen of these establishments insisted upon maintaining excellent quality – an important point for the would-be collector to remember when buying pieces.

COMPLETE SETS
Complete canteens are probably the best items to look out for in a trade where parts of services are all too easy to find. Their survival is relatively uncommon, however, and care should be taken to find examples in their original boxes. These are often made of oak, and sometimes carry their trade labels. They are usually lined, with green or blue baize for the English market, and chamois for the Scottish.

Collecting individual pieces of table silver and cutlery here and there to form your own canteen can, of course, offer its own rewards as dealers in second-hand silver have known for many years. But a word of warning is necessary for the inexperienced, particularly where a popular pattern such as King's is concerned. Where a number of different manufacturers produced the same

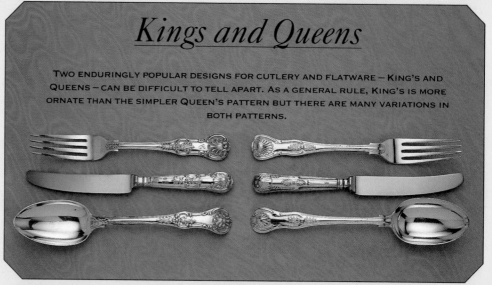

Kings and Queens

TWO ENDURINGLY POPULAR DESIGNS FOR CUTLERY AND FLATWARE – KING'S AND QUEENS – CAN BE DIFFICULT TO TELL APART. AS A GENERAL RULE, KING'S IS MORE ORNATE THAN THE SIMPLER QUEEN'S PATTERN BUT THERE ARE MANY VARIATIONS IN BOTH PATTERNS.

Fish Slice and Fork

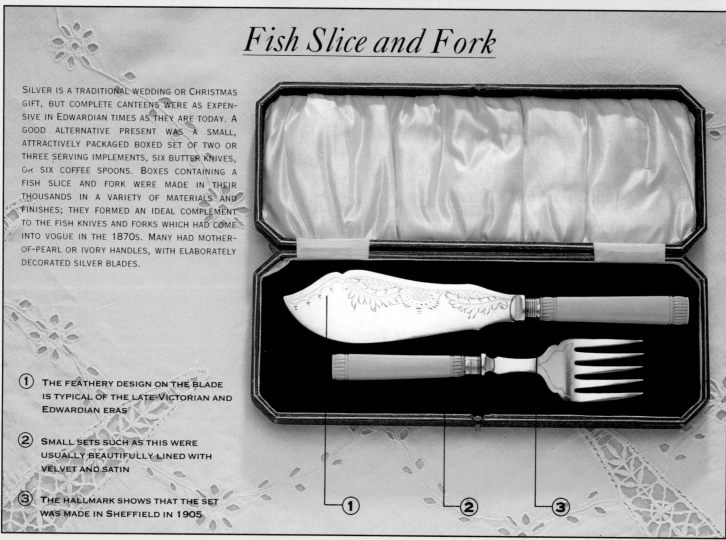

SILVER IS A TRADITIONAL WEDDING OR CHRISTMAS GIFT, BUT COMPLETE CANTEENS WERE AS EXPENSIVE IN EDWARDIAN TIMES AS THEY ARE TODAY. A GOOD ALTERNATIVE PRESENT WAS A SMALL, ATTRACTIVELY PACKAGED BOXED SET OF TWO OR THREE SERVING IMPLEMENTS, SIX BUTTER KNIVES, OR SIX COFFEE SPOONS. BOXES CONTAINING A FISH SLICE AND FORK WERE MADE IN THEIR THOUSANDS IN A VARIETY OF MATERIALS AND FINISHES; THEY FORMED AN IDEAL COMPLEMENT TO THE FISH KNIVES AND FORKS WHICH HAD COME INTO VOGUE IN THE 1870s. MANY HAD MOTHER-OF-PEARL OR IVORY HANDLES, WITH ELABORATELY DECORATED SILVER BLADES.

① THE FEATHERY DESIGN ON THE BLADE IS TYPICAL OF THE LATE-VICTORIAN AND EDWARDIAN ERAS

② SMALL SETS SUCH AS THIS WERE USUALLY BEAUTIFULLY LINED WITH VELVET AND SATIN

③ THE HALLMARK SHOWS THAT THE SET WAS MADE IN SHEFFIELD IN 1905

·CLOSE UP·

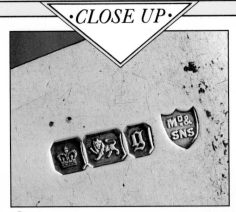

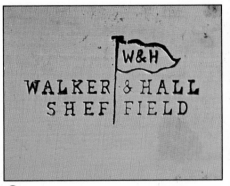

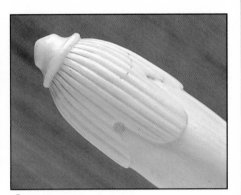

① **HALLMARK WITH MAKER'S MARK**

② **ELECTROPLATED FLATWARE**

③ **MAKER'S MARK WITH HALLMARK**

④ **WALKER AND HALL TRADEMARK**

⑤ **ENGRAVED AND BRIGHT-CUT DECORATION**

⑥ **CARVED IVORY HANDLE**

① THE MARKS SHOW THE FORK WAS MADE IN 1899 BY MAXFIELD AND SONS

④ THE STEEL BLADE OF A CARVER BEARS THE NAME OF ITS MAKER

② MANY PIECES MADE IN EPNS ARE MARKED AS SUCH

⑤ NOVELTY OBJECTS LIKE JAM SPOONS ARE OFTEN HIGHLY ORNATE

③ THIS PIECE FROM 1912 CARRIES THE MARK OF JOHN ROUND AND SON LTD

⑥ MANY SERVING IMPLEMENTS HAVE FINELY CARVED HANDLES

pattern over many years, slight variations were inevitable; take care in matching the design exactly. Ideally, purchasers should select items all made in the same place and at the same time. On the other hand, pieces of Lily pattern, for example, a design exclusive to Elkington & Co. Ltd of Birmingham, will always be identical but it was made in much smaller quantities and is therefore more difficult to find.

EASY AVAILABILITY

In general, none of the main articles of an Edwardian canteen – the table knives, spoons and forks, the dessert spoons and forks and teaspoons – should be difficult to acquire. Other items, such as salt spoons, soup spoons, fish knives and forks, sugar sifters and tongs, as well as large serving spoons, soup ladles and fish servers, are also readily available. Less easy to find are the luxury pieces used for dessert courses. These richly designed items, often made of gilt, include ice cream spoons and servers with their characteristic shovel-shaped bowls, which first appear to have been used in the 1880s.

The table silver which is usually associated with tea time, or with the serving of fruit salad, more properly comes under the heading of 'novelties' and would require a chapter all of its own. The many hundreds of designs which were made for our Victorian and Edwardian ancestors make a fascinating study, none more so than the pieces originally created especially for Liberty's of Regent Street. Their teaspoons, and similar items made in the fashionable art nouveau style, were sometimes enamelled in attractive peacock colours.

At the beginning of this century, silver-handled steel and silver-bladed and pronged knives or forks began to be made with 'lockfast' handles: the two elements of each – the blade or prongs and the handle – were soldered to one another to form a solid joint. Knives and forks not made in this way included examples with old-fashioned pitch-filled handles or those with handles of mother-of-pearl or ivory.

POINTS TO WATCH

■ Make sure you know whether you are buying solid silver or EPNS (electroplated nickel silver), which should be cheaper.

■ Watch for minor variations in the same pattern produced by different manufacturers if you are aiming to complete a set.

■ Pieces with pitch-filled, ivory or mother-of-pearl handles should never be totally submerged in water, as this will cause their internal adhesives to disintegrate.

■ Steel blades (as opposed to stainless steel ones) can be dangerously sharp. Wash with care and dry immediately, and slightly grease before storing in greaseproof paper.

▶ *During the Victorian and Edwardian eras several items of tableware were patented whose precise function has now been forgotten. This small spoon is one example – it may have been used for food that needed straining.*

Dressing-table Silver

The Victorian dressing table sparkled with a glittering array of
silver accessories, which formed an essential part of the daily
beauty routine and added glamour to the bedroom

S ilver accessories for the dressing table
have long been as much a pleasure to
use as an important decorative feature
of the bedroom. The more elaborate sets,
presented in attractive cases and ostenta-
tiously decorated or engraved with a
monogram or crest, were also a powerful
status symbol.

While the most modest Victorian vanity
sets consisted of a small number of basic
grooming implements, the most comprehen-
sive neglected no aspect of the beauty
routine. Indeed, from hair brush to shoe
horn, the 30 or so items that went to make
up the largest vanity sets enabled the
Victorian woman to groom herself, literally,
from head to toe. Men's needs were
similarly well catered for; an array of 20
items neatly packed into a case took care of
most eventualities.

EARLY SETS

Dressing-table sets first became fashionable
amongst the wealthy between the 1670s and
the first decade of the 18th century, and
some fine examples survive from this period.
Fashioned in silver or silver gilt, their
component parts were expensive versions of
toilet articles that already existed in brass,
pewter or humble pottery. The whole set,
dominated by a large mirror and candlesticks, with a number of bowls and boxes,
was often richly embossed to create an
opulent effect.

Simpler services continued to be made
during the middle and later years of the 18th
century, but they suffered a general decline
in popularity. It was not until the 1790s that
they were manufactured in quantity. Even
then, the dressing-table set was considered
to be a luxury item, presumably because it
was so expensive.

VICTORIAN TASTE

By the beginning of the 19th century, silver
dressing-table sets were coming back into
fashion, and after 1815 many were sold
tidily boxed in dressing cases. During the
Victorian era, the trend was for sets to
contain smaller but more numerous pieces,
with a variety of cut-glass bottles to hold
creams and lotions, hair and clothes
brushes, and several other accessories.

A mass market in dressing-table sets
developed during the Victorian period and

they rapidly became an affordable luxury.
The majority of the boxed sets were
produced in London, Sheffield and Birmingham. Important makers included Mappin and Webb in London and Sheffield,
who produced complete sets from the 1840s
onwards, Aspreys, and Walker and Hall.

Many sets consisted of pieces made by
several different silversmiths who specialized

▲ *An ornate Victorian dressing table is adorned
with a sumptuous display of accessories in cut
glass and richly-decorated silver.*

in particular accessories: William Comyns
and Sons of London, for instance, were
prolific makers of dressing-table trays and
elaborately decorated silver-mounted cologne bottles, while other workshops sup-

plied items such as spoons and vinaigrettes. There were also silversmiths specializing in particular branches of smallwork; these included mounters, piercers, chasers and engravers.

The manufacture of the boxed sets involved numerous other trades. There were the cabinet makers who produced high quality wooden cases, one of the most celebrated being George Betjemann and Sons of Pentonville Road, who supplied firms such as Aspreys with their boxes. Velvet and silk linings for the cases came from fabric manufacturers, and the locks and keys to close them were produced by specialist locksmiths. Mother-of-pearl and ivory workers supplied additional decoration for the boxes and their contents; and the services of enamellers and mounters of precious and semi-precious stones would also have been called upon when needed. Glass makers and cutters made the bottles for the sets; metal workers provided corkscrews for scent bottles, razors and knife blades; gilders provided some of the internal mounts and auxiliary fittings, such as gilt-metal mirrors.

MATERIALS AND TECHNIQUES

The vanity sets produced at the height of the Victorian era came in wooden cases of varying quality, and in different finishes, to suit every pocket. At the top end of the market were cases made from coromandel wood inlaid with brass (sometimes with ingeniously hinged sections or trays), while cheaper cases were made from mahogany-veneered softwood. The fittings also came in every quality: some were produced in richly chased gold with enamel or coral and split pearl monograms, or with silver, Sheffield plate or electroplate decoration.

During the late 1870s and 1880s the wooden cases for dressing sets were gradually superseded by those made of leather. At first, these were soft, rather squashy 'Gladstone bags', but these soon gave way to the stiff rectangular versions.

For the bottles and boxes inside, solid silver was, of course, the material chosen for the best and most expensive sets. The methods of decoration ranged from hand chasing and hand engraving to repoussé work. However, more economical materials and decorative techniques were used for the vast majority of mass-produced sets.

When the design required rich chasing, makers soon found that hand work was too expensive, and turned instead to die-stamped work. This involved pressing thin sheets of silver known as blanks, in powerful machines between two engraved steel dies, one negative and one positive, to reproduce a given design. The resulting shells were then trimmed, assembled, and in the case of large items like hairbrushes, filled with pitch to give them bulk and strength.

Virtually all English die-stamped work was carried out in Birmingham and Sheffield workshops, which had the necessary heavy machinery. A firm like William Comyns and Sons of London was in the habit of ordering large numbers of these die-stamped shells, and assembling them in their own workshops for eventual distribution to retail outlets like Boots the Chemists. From the end of the 19th century, much die-stamping work was also carried out in Germany, France and the United States.

Electroplating, the process by which a fine coat of silver was fused on to a base metal such as nickel, was another revolutionary economy measure widely exploited at the time in order to produce less expensive silverware.

ABUNDANT DECORATION

Typical decoration conformed to High Victorian taste for the ornate, and included profuse clusters of flowers, buds and leaves, neo-Rococo shells and scrolls, and cherubs peering over clouds. Fine tracery also decorated the lids of some bowls and boxes. Towards the end of the century, progressive shops such as Liberty's began to stock dressing-table silver in the art nouveau style, with floral and foliate relief designs.

Millions of toilet sets were produced from the 1880s up to World War I. The war did not completely put a stop to production of silverware, even though some of the larger die-stamping machines were reserved for making soldiers' helmets, and

▲ *The wealthy Victorian woman had plenty of time for an elaborate beauty routine, and the variety of accessories available reflected the importance she placed on grooming.*

many factories went over to munitions, but the trade was drastically curtailed and never really recovered. World War II all but ended the manufacture of silver in England, especially the trinket and accessory market, which had thrived throughout Victorian and Edwardian times.

COMPARISONS

The Dorset Service

THIS SILVER-GILT DRESSING-TABLE SET DECORATED WITH PASTORAL SCENES AND FAMILY CREST, WAS GIVEN BY THE 1ST DUKE OF DORSET TO HIS DAUGHTER ON HER MARRIAGE IN 1742.

Women's Dressing-Table Accessories

The principal items in a woman's matching vanity set were a hair brush, comb, hand-mirror and clothes brush. The most basic sets consisted only of these items. Larger sets included, in addition, an array of silver-topped or silver-mounted cut-glass jars and bottles for lavender water, eau-de-cologne, rouge and face powder. Larger sets still also contained jewellery boxes, manicure equipment, pin trays, hair tidies, a pair of miniature candlesticks and an easel-support mirror. In the most luxurious, a full manicure set and writing equipment would be found.

The Victorian dressing table was, however, incomplete without several other elegant aids to dressing. There were, for instance, silver-handled curling tongs, bonnet brushes, glove stretchers and silver glove-powderers and, smallest but perhaps most useful, silver-handled button hooks.

Further silver items on the dressing table – not always part of the vanity set – might be a ring tree, frequently in the shape of an actual tree – a pot pourri and, perhaps, a 'novelty' perfume bottle in an original shape.

▲ *A selection of cut-glass silver-topped bottles and containers for powders and pins. The long bottle would have been used for cologne.*

PRICE GUIDE ❹ ❺

PRICE GUIDE

▶ *An 1883 serpentine silver clothes brush adorned with bucolic scenes.*

PRICE GUIDE ❺

◀ *An Edwardian trinket box with Art Nouveau embellishment.*

PRICE GUIDE ❺

▲ *A 1914 clothes brush with high relief decoration showing three angelic faces.*

PRICE GUIDE ❷

▶ *A small rouge pot from 1889, with Rococo decoration on the silver lid.*

PRICE GUIDE ❸

▲ *A rare example of two silver-topped scent bottles in a silver-plated stand.*

PRICE GUIDE ❺

▶ *This silver perfume bottle, dating from 1890, would have been kept in a handbag.*

PRICE GUIDE ❺

▲ *A Victorian die-stamped silver hand mirror, with typically florid decoration.*

PRICE GUIDE ❹

▲ *An attractive Edwardian scent bottle with silver mounted on blue glass.*

PRICE GUIDE ❺

▶ *A bonnet brush with a silver handle, from about 1900.*

PRICE GUIDE ❸

Men's Silver Accessories

oilet accessories for men contained in a fitted case made the ideal travelling set, and many such sets were made for military officers.

Like women's vanity sets, the gentleman's travelling set consisted of a surprisingly large number of jars and bottles, although these held pomade and oils rather than creams and face powder. Larger sets accommodated up to ten such vessels. There were also hair brushes – handleless and supplied in pairs – manicure items and even a jewellery case.

The really distinctive feature of a man's dressing set was, of course, the shaving equipment. This consisted of a silver mug or beaker, a silver-mounted brush, a razor strop and cut-throat razors with silver clip-on safety guards.

Small curling tongs – smaller than those for women's hair – were also included, to groom luxuriant beards and moustaches, and there was often a small spirit burner on which they could be warmed. Shoe horns and boot pulls, and a spirit flask or two, with a detachable silver cup, completed the set.

Men's dressing sets differed from women's vanity sets not merely because of their contents. Their decoration tended to be much more restrained, sometimes consisting only of a plain engraved or stamped initial.

▼ *The cologne bottle from the late-Victorian toilet set (below right)*

PRICE GUIDE ④

▶ *A late-Victorian talcum powder container, with an initial on the lid.*

PRICE GUIDE ④

▼ *A late-Victorian cologne bottle. Most gentleman's sets would have contained several of these.*

PRICE GUIDE ④

▶ *Two silver hair tidies from 1897, used for storing hair removed from brushes.*

PRICE GUIDE ③

▶ *An Edwardian silver-topped glass box used for tie pins and other accessories.*

PRICE GUIDE ④

PRICE GUIDE

◀ A silver match
container and striker,
with a stand for the
lighted match.

PRICE GUIDE **5**

◀ A late-Victorian
silver ring box of
pleasingly simple
design.

PRICE GUIDE **5**

▲ Two silver and
crystal pots – one for
pomade, the other for
a shaving brush.

PRICE GUIDE **4**

▲ A silver clothes
brush from c. 1900 –
decoration consists of
a simple border.

PRICE GUIDE **3**

▲ Bottles with
matching silver lids,
from an 1890s
gentleman's toilet set.

PRICE GUIDE **4**

COLLECTOR'S TIPS

The amount and variety of dressing-table silver produced throughout Victorian times provides enormous scope for today's collector, and much of it is quite affordable. A wide range of Victorian dressing-table silver will be found on specialist silver stands at antiques centres and markets, and at antiques fairs.

The majority of items of dressing-table silver for sale today are separate pieces from what were once large sets. Complete sets are rarer and often more expensive than the sum of their parts. Those still in their beautifully inlaid, velvet-lined wooden case – a delight to own and use – command the highest prices.

USEFUL COLLECTABLES

Among individual or paired pieces of dressing-table silver, those that still have a use on today's dressing tables are the most keenly sought after. At the top of the range of the more accessible pieces are large cut-glass and silver bottles; those sold in pairs, as well as those with a decorative silver casing, are particularly desirable.

Smaller silver-topped bottles, sold singly or in groups of two, three or more, are less expensive but still very collectable. Shaving equipment and soap boxes, picture frames and small mirrors, ring trees and trinket boxes also fall into the middle range. Brushes are less in demand, and can offer a bargain to the interested collector.

Pieces which are rarely used today, generally, though by no means always, form the most inexpensive collecting areas. Hair tidies and hatpin holders, glove stretchers and glove hooks, curling tongs, bonnet brushes and the cheap and ubiquitous button hooks, all fall into this category and, depending on the materials they are made from, can be acquired for modest sums. Razors, by contrast, though unusable today, are more expensive than most other outmoded toilet equipment.

Individual pieces from manicure sets are also good value: silver-handled nail files, nail cleaners, dainty pairs of scissors and nail polishers are plentiful and easy to collect. Complete manicure sets in their cases are more expensive.

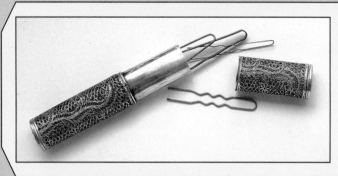

Hairpin Holder

THE VICTORIANS INVENTED A VAST NUMBER OF GROOMING AIDS. THIS SMALL SILVER FILIGREE TUBE WAS SPECIFICALLY DESIGNED TO HOLD HAIRPINS.

The Boxed Grooming Set

BOXED SETS CONTAINING DIFFERENT GROOMING IMPLEMENTS WERE MADE IN LARGE QUANTITIES DURING THE VICTORIAN PERIOD. WHILE SOME WERE PART OF LARGER TOILET SETS, MANY WERE MADE SEPARATELY, AND WERE PRESENTED IN THEIR OWN LEATHER OR CROCODILE FITTED CASES LINED WITH VELVET OR SATIN. MOST PIECES WERE HIGHLY ORNATE, WITH TYPICAL DECORATION CONSISTING OF SCROLLING LEAVES AND FLOWERS. PLAINER ACCESSORIES WITH UNDECORATED HANDLES ARE FAR RARER.

THIS MID-VICTORIAN SET CONTAINS THREE PIECES OF EQUIPMENT THAT A LADY WOULD HAVE FOUND VERY USEFUL WHILE SHE WAS DRESSING — A SHOE HORN, A BUTTON HOOK AND CURLING TONGS.

(1) THE BASE OF THE CASE IS RIGID, AND EACH PIECE SITS IN ITS ALLOCATED NICHE.

(2) SIGNS OF WEAR AND TEAR CAN BE SEEN ON THE CURLING TONGS, WHICH HAVE BEEN BLACKENED FROM CONSTANT USE.

(3) THE HIGH RELIEF DECORATION IS TYPICAL OF THE EFFECT PRODUCED BY DIE CASTING.

(4) THE CASE IS COVERED IN MAROON LEATHER. THIS IS THE PART THAT USUALLY SHOWS THE MOST OBVIOUS SIGNS OF DAMAGE.

◁ CLOSE UP ▷

① FINE TRACERY

② HINGED CAP

③ WEAR AND TEAR

① SOME SCENT BOTTLES HAVE A FINE TRACERY OF SILVER LAID OVER GLASS.

② THE TOP OF THE SMELLING SALTS BOTTLE FLIPS BACK TO ALLOW THE SALTS TO BE PLACED INSIDE THE CAP.

③ CONSTANT USE HAS ERODED DETAIL AND CAUSED HOLES TO DEVELOP IN THIS LID.

④ THE HOLLOW UNDERSIDE OF A LID REVEALS THAT DIE STAMPING HAS BEEN USED TO PRODUCE HIGH RELIEF DECORATION.

⑤ THE HALLMARK ON THE BASE OF THIS SCENT BOTTLE SHOWS THAT IT WAS MADE IN BIRMINGHAM IN 1902.

⑥ MANY SILVER ACCESSORIES WERE PERSONALIZED BY A MONOGRAM.

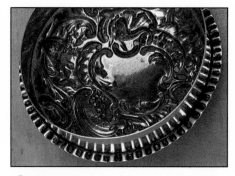

④ DIE STAMPING

⑤ HALLMARK

⑥ MONOGRAM

The best quality pieces are made from solid silver and a hallmark on each piece will indicate the maker, the year and place of manufacture and the quality of silver used. However, the majority of affordable pieces will be of thin die-stamped silver, or electroplate.

DECORATIVE DETAILS

Decoration in the form of engraving or repoussé work can add interest and value to a piece, but many collectors prefer the uniform ripple effect of spot hammering over the entire surface of, say, a soap box or ointment jar to overblown ornament in high relief.

The presence of a *discreet* monogram should not greatly affect value either way. Some collectors, however, find this off-putting, and it should be borne in mind that a monogram or other unwanted decoration cannot be erased from very thin silver without disastrous results.

Thin sheets of silver on the lids of boxes and bowls, or on the backs of brushes and hand mirrors, often show signs of wear. Over-polishing and decades of daily handling wear away the detail on engraved or embossed pieces and are especially damag-ing to electroplate. Worn engraving or the appearance of the base metal through the coat of silver are common signs of wear. Holes may appear on raised areas of embossed decoration, particularly if the silver is thin. A rattling noise in a hand mirror or brush indicates that the pitch backing has dried and fragmented.

LIDS AND HINGES

When buying silver-topped bottles, it is important to check that screw-top lids still fit securely and that hinged lids have not broken. Missing glass stoppers, which provided an air-tight seal beneath the silver top, can be replaced, although this is obviously an additional expense. A good restorer will be able to replace worn bristles in brushes. Replacing blackened or blemished silvering in mirrors, however, tends to devalue them.

Once a small set of matching dressing-table silver has been acquired – and it is important to check that the pieces really do match – an interesting way to continue is to seek out other similar pieces to extend the set. With luck and diligence, it may just be possible to find a piece or two made to exactly the same pattern.

POINTS TO WATCH

■ Check items such as lids and trays for holes caused by wear, by holding them up to the light.

■ Badly worn or damaged pieces can be difficult to repair and should be avoided.

■ An inscription or crest may add value to a piece; a prominent monogram may detract from it.

■ Check vulnerable hinges on boxes, flasks and bottles for strain.

■ Every genuine piece of silver should have a hallmark.

▲ *A silver manicure set in its case, complete with nail buffer and pot for polishing powder.*

Bronzes

Bronze is an ideal metal for casting and has long been worked
by sculptors and foundries around the world. But the best
Victorian bronze animals and figures came from France,
Austria and the Orient

Bronze is an alloy of copper and tin.
Its relatively low melting point made
it one of the first metals to be used in
the manufacture of weapons and utensils. It
has also been the customary medium for
metal sculpture for more than 4000 years.

Bronze is particularly suitable for the
casting of finely made statuary. As it
solidifies, it expands, forcing the metal into
every crevice of the mould. Then, as it cools
down, bronze contracts slightly, facilitating
separation from the mould.

The method of casting called 'lost-wax
casting' (or *cire perdu*) remained the
favoured system for producing fine work,
but in the 19th century electrotyping was
also introduced. This was a process involving electrolysis and the depositing of a very
thin layer of bronze on the face of a mould.
The result was a flood of accurate and much
cheaper metalwork that decorated the
homes of the 19th-century bourgeoisie.

From Italy came quantities of 'after the
antique' statuary, inspired by the archaeolo-
gical discoveries at Pompeii and Hercula-
neum. Much of this was of good quality and
remains extremely collectable today.

LEADING FRENCH SCULPTORS

More interesting perhaps was a new departure in bronze sculpture by Antoine-Louis
Barye (1796-1875). Barye started work as
an apprentice to a goldsmith, but soon
began sculpting animal figures. In his search
for realism he studied the anatomy of
animals by dissecting corpses. The result
was a series of vigorous, finely-made animal
bronzes. Although success came late –
Barye was bankrupted at one point and had
to enter into partnership with Emile Martin
– Barye is now recognized as one of the
major Romantic artists of the 19th century.

Barye opened his own bronze foundry,
and cast many of his models himself. These,
and those cast by his assistant Gonon and
his sons, were of extremely high quality.

Skilled at modelling animals, Barye was
not always so successful with human figures.
He also made candelabra and clocks which
were often decorated with animals, and he
was particularly proficient in the colouring

Italian Neptune

THIS EXQUISITE GILT-BRONZE STATUETTE
OF NEPTUNE WAS MADE IN VENICE IN
THE 16TH CENTURY. THE GOD OF THE SEA
IS STANDING OVER ONE OF HIS SUBJECTS
– A FISH.

and patination of bronzes. The result of Barye's success was the establishment of the school of *animaliers* in France, which included Emmanuel Frémiet, Auguste-Nicolas Cain, Georges Gardet and Pierre-Jules Mêne.

By the middle of the 19th century 6000 men were employed in Paris in the manufacture of popular decorative bronzes. It was now a big commercial business, and the sculptors frequently did no more than provide models for the bronze-founders and finishers. Much of this work was shown at the annual salons in Paris.

VARIED SUBJECT MATTER

The French sculptor Jules Dalou, who fled to England as a political refugee in 1871, made figures derived from the popular paintings of Jean François Millet, and started a fashion for bronzes of peasants. Other favourite subjects of the time included allegorical figures and groups. There were busts of Shakespeare, Napoleon and Mary Queen of Scots, and statuettes of the Prince of Wales, the Duke of Wellington and of boys playing catch. Highly ornate candlesticks and candelabra

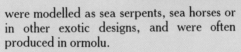

▶ *In this sentimental painting, entitled* The Wedding Gown, *the background articles are all typically Victorian in style and feel. The heavy bronze statuette of a medieval knight stands upon a deeply carved piece of furniture, beside a painting with a large, ornate frame. The interest in the Middle Ages, shown in the subject matter of the statuette, was a feature of Victorian art.*

◀▼ *Nineteenth-century bronzes exhibited a wide range of subject matter – mythological characters, such as the winged Mercury, figures from ancient and modern history, and bird and animal bronzes were all popular.*

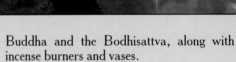

were modelled as sea serpents, sea horses or in other exotic designs, and were often produced in ormolu.

DECORATING BRONZES

The word 'ormolu' comes from the French *or moulu* meaning 'powdered gold'. It was used extensively for decoration, especially on 18th- and 19th-century French furniture. Originally the coating was applied by a mercuric process but this involved the release of poisonous fumes. The famous Florentine sculptor of the 16th century, Benvenuto Cellini, advised in his treatise that the sculptor should find someone else to do this work for him! But in the 19th century a method was devised of applying gold dust in varnish, a much safer process.

Another method of decorating bronzes was cold-painting. This was practised especially in Vienna in the 19th century, but was popular throughout Europe. Cold-painted figures and busts were produced, as well as the ever-popular animals.

EASTERN ART

Oriental bronzes form a fascinating and broad field. Chinese bronze workers were skilled in their art many centuries before those in Europe. Bronzes continued to be made in the traditional style in 19th-century China, with many figures of the seated Buddha and the Bodhisattva, along with incense burners and vases.

The Japanese bronzes of the Meiji period (1868-1912) also included some very fine work. Trumpeting elephants with ivory tusks were particularly popular, along with animal groups and Japanese figures. All these oriental bronzes would have been found on sale in the London stores during the 19th-century vogue for Japonisme, which started when Japan's frontiers were reopened to the West after 1854.

BRITISH SCULPTORS

After about 1870 there was a revival of the so-called Renaissance style, involving the casting of such items as large, highly-decorated jugs and ewers. Later the British sculptor Alfred Gilbert (whose best-known piece is Piccadilly's Eros) produced several bronze statuettes, many of them in a style that foreshadowed Art Nouveau.

The few bronzes made by George Frederick Watts, who is better known as a painter, are also worth noting. He studied in the studio of William Behnes, and produced some fine busts and allegorical figures, as well as larger public work. But generally speaking little of importance was made in bronze in England, and therefore people decorated their drawing rooms with the work of European sculptors.

Animals

Animals were perhaps the single most popular subject for decorative bronzes in the mid-19th century. The French school of *animaliers* produced figures of chamois, horses, lions, dogs, deer with fawns, lionesses carrying cubs, and many, many more.

Particularly notable among its work were the bronzes of Antoine-Louis Barye depicting animal combats. These are well-conceived and executed with great spirit, and had a clear influence on the great French sculptor Auguste Rodin.

Of the many bronzes depicting horses, P. J. Mêne's *Vainqueur de Derby* is a good example, while Alfred, Count d'Orsay's *Duke of Wellington on Horseback* appealed greatly to the patriotic British. Oriental animal bronzes were of more exotic animals, such as tigers

and elephants. They also produced lion-shaped censers.

There is, of course, a clear link between the paintings of Sir Edwin Landseer, which depicted animals in highly sentimental terms, and the *animalier* mountain goats that graced the sideboards of many Victorian homes. Landseer, it should not be forgotten, also modelled the four lions at the base of Nelson's Column in Trafalgar Square.

Less appealing to some modern tastes, but amusing for all that, are the Viennese miniature bronzes of cats. They are cold-painted, as was usual with Austrian bronzes, and depict cats fencing, boxing and drinking champagne. Christie's recently sold a collection of some seventy of these rather kitsch sculptures and they fetched over £6500!

▼ *This striking mare and foal dates from around 1840, and was executed by Christophe Fratin (1800-64). The over-thin appearance of the mare, with her protruding ribs, is characteristic of Fratin's work. He was taught by the great Romantic painter and sculptor Géricault.*

PRICE GUIDE **9**

▼ *A small bronze fox by Prosper Lecourtier (1855-94) is dated 1875. Lecourtier's animals are always sensitively modelled.*

PRICE GUIDE **8**

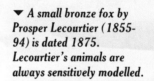

▼ *Pheasants and other birds were popular subjects among the animalier sculptors. Moigniez was undoubtedly the greatest bird sculptor of the 19th century, but many others also excelled. This piece is by Mêne.*

PRICE GUIDE **8**

◀ *This wild goat bronze by Jules Moigniez (1835-94) was exhibited in the Paris Salon of 1867. The French sculptor's work was very popular in England and Scotland.*

PRICE GUIDE **8**

PRICE GUIDE

▶ *This portrait of the famous jockey Fred Archer on his Derby winning mount 'Bienore' was presented as the prize for the 1876 Course des Saintes horse race. It was executed by Pierre Jules Mêne, one of the most commercially successful animal sculptors of his day.*

PRICE GUIDE **9**

▼ *Dogs are probably second only to horses in popularity, and are generally much cheaper to collect. This fine sculpture by Moigniez shows a bassett hound standing on rocky ground. It dates from around 1870.*

PRICE GUIDE **8**

◀ *One group of bronzes depicts animals – particularly monkeys and bears – with human characteristics. Fratin was a master in this field. This seated bear, reading and smoking a pipe (c. 1850) has the ironic humour typical of the genre.*

PRICE GUIDE **8**

Figures

The most common subjects for bronze figures of this period are probably the reproductions of classical statuary and mythological figures. Gods and goddesses, Baccantes, nymphs and water-carriers were all popular.

Then there were contemporary and historical characters either full-length or as a bust. Napoleon appeared frequently, but so did Florence Nightingale, Rousseau, Voltaire, Shakespeare, Milton, Alexander Pope and Mary Queen of Scots, to name but a few.

Among the mythological subjects, Cupid and Psyche were popular, and were modelled as bronze torchères (candle-stands), as well as simple figures. Barye's *Roger and Angelica borne by the Hippogriff* is a notable mythological group.

Arab figures were common as well, and were sometimes mounted, sometimes not. A number of bronzes depict Arabs engaged in falconry. Among the cold-painted Austrian bronzes one finds the dancing figures of Whirling Dervishes, the mystic Turkish Moslem sect which was suppressed by Ataturk. These Middle Eastern subjects, together with the Japanese bronze figures and the Chinese Buddhas of the period, demonstrate the obsession of the time with all things eastern.

The other major group of bronze figures of this period are the male and female nudes. Once again the subject was often of a classical nature. Some of the more risqué bronzes of satyrs and nymphs and nude female figures betray the veiled Victorian fascination with sex.

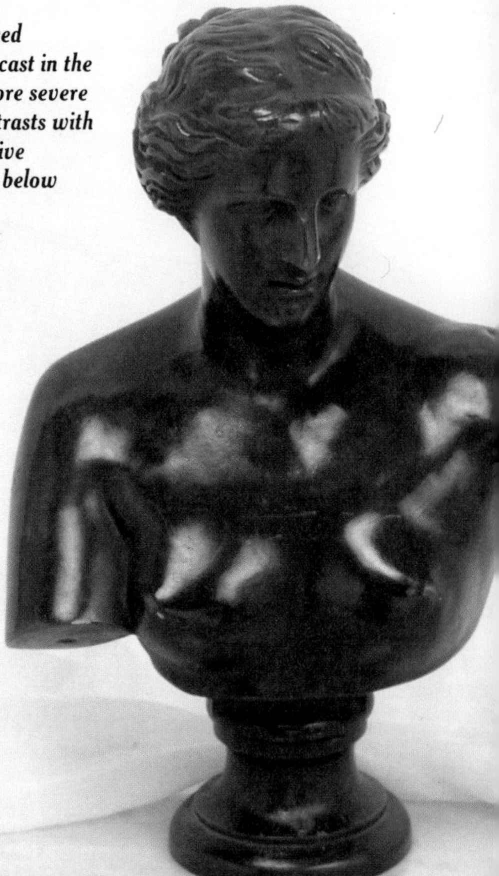

▶ *A classical bust of a naked female figure, which was cast in the mid-19th century. The more severe classicism of this bust contrasts with the prettier, more decorative qualities of the two pieces below and on the left.*

PRICE GUIDE **6**

◀ *Many Victorian bronzes hark back to ancient sculpture. This small, hollow-cast bronze, executed towards the end of the 19th century, shows a classically dressed woman, standing with her hands raised to her hair.*

PRICE GUIDE **4**

◀ *This seated female figure with a lyre is depicted in a classic pose — with her chin resting in her hand, in pensive mood. It is a beautiful piece, executed in the mid-19th century. Probably the mosr famous example of this pensive pose is Auguste Rodin's The Thinker.*

PRICE GUIDE **7**

▼ The bearded male nude, with his arm raised, was one of the many mythological figures which adorned 19th-century drawing rooms. More sexually titillating examples were also popular with apparently straight-laced Victorian collectors.

PRICE GUIDE **6**

▼ This magnificent bust in the Chinese style was sculpted by Jean Baptiste Carpeaux (1827-75) in the 1860s. It is by far the most expensive work on this page – Carpeaux was one of the most important French sculptors of his day. The golden patina on the face is particularly striking.

PRICE GUIDE **9**

▲ Another group of classical figures popular in the 19th century were Greek or Roman scholars. This Greek scholar, one of a pair, dates from between 1870 and 1890.

PRICE GUIDE **7**

COLLECTOR'S TIPS

All copper alloys corrode readily, and bronze is no exception. In extreme cases the corrosion can proceed to a point where the tin separates from the copper, but usually the effects of corrosion do not penetrate much below the surface. The surface corrosion on old bronzes was deliberately effected by bronze sculptors of the 19th century to give a pleasing colour to the work, and replace the brassy hues of unfinished bronze.

Patination is sometimes removed to reveal inlaying or an inscription, but this is quite unusual. Generally it should be left untouched, because if cleaned – even with the mildest of detergents – it will be damaged and become patchy.

Judging the date of a bronze by its patina is a matter of great expertise and requires experience. Part of the skill, especially of the French craftsmen of the 19th century, was in the finishing of their bronzes with colour and patination. However, modern bronze statues often have their surfaces coloured with chemicals or paint, so the collector should remember that appearances can be deceptive.

The 19th century was the great period of reproductions, so for a collector it is usually more a matter of discerning between an older original and a 19th-century copy, than between a Victorian bronze and a modern copy. However, it should be remembered that a great quantity of reproduction metalware of all kinds was made between the wars, some of which may now have acquired some patination.

Having said that, there are other helpful indications for those interested in 19th-century bronzes. Most obviously, many

COMPARISONS

Patination

THE COLOURS USED TO PATINATE BRONZES VARY FROM SCULPTOR TO SCULPTOR. BARYE PREFERRED DARK GREENS WHILE MOIGNIEZ FAVOURED BLACK, OR ON OCCASIONS, GILT. A REPATINATED EXAMPLE WILL RARELY HAVE THE SAME DEPTH OF COLOUR AS AN OLD BRONZE, AS PATINATION TAKES MANY YEARS TO BECOME STABLE.

Barye Fils Bronze

ALFRED BARYE WAS THE SON OF THE CELEBRATED FRENCH ANIMAL SCULPTOR ANTOINE-LOUIS BARYE. HE WAS TRAINED BY HIS FATHER AND, LIKE HIM, SPECIALIZED IN ANIMAL SUBJECTS. INDEED, HE OFTEN TRIED TO CAPITALIZE ON THE CONFUSION THAT COULD ARISE FROM TWO SCULPTORS CALLED A. BARYE WORKING IN THE SAME FIELD. AT FIRST, HE SIGNED HIS PIECES 'A. BARYE', OR 'BARYE'. ON HIS FATHER'S INSISTENCE HE CHANGED HIS SIGNATURE: 'A. BARYE FILS' (FILS IS FRENCH FOR 'SON') IS THE MOST COMMON. WHEN ALFRED STOOPED TO PRESENTING BILLS TO HIS FATHER'S CLIENTS AND POCKETING THE MONEY, HE WAS OBLIGED TO LEAVE HOME, AND ANTOINE-LOUIS BROKE OFF ALL CONTACT WITH HIM. HE MAY NOT HAVE BEEN AS GREAT AN ARTIST AS HIS FATHER BUT WAS AN EXTREMELY SKILLED SCULPTOR IN HIS OWN RIGHT, PRODUCING MANY FINELY WORKED ANIMAL PIECES — PARTICULARLY RACEHORSES, DOGS AND PARTRIDGES.

THIS LITTLE BRONZE SHOWS CLEOPATRA RIDING ON AN ELEPHANT, WITH ITS FOOT ON THE HEAD OF THE SPHINX. IT WAS MADE AROUND 1870.

① THE BASE IS DECORATED WITH A STYLIZED LEAF PATTERN. BARYE'S SIGNATURE APPEARS TWICE ON THE TOP.

② A WARM BROWN PATINA IS CHARACTERISTIC OF BARYE FILS' WORK.

③ THERE IS FINE ATTENTION TO NATURALISTIC DETAIL.

④ NOTE THE LIVELY SENSE OF MOVEMENT IN BARYE FILS' ANIMALS.

CLOSE UP

① PIERRE-JULES MÊNE

② JEAN BAPTISTE CARPEAUX

③ JULES MOIGNIEZ

④ SITES FOR WEAR

⑤ PATINATION

⑥ INTRICATE DETAIL

① A SIGNATURE CAN BE 'ALL IMPORTANT' ON A BRONZE – PIERRE-JULES MÊNE, THE MOST SUCCESSFUL ANIMALIER OF HIS DAY, DIED IN 1871.

④ BRONZE WHICH IS CONSTANTLY STROKED OR TOUCHED SHOWS OBVIOUS WEAR, AS SEEN ON THIS BUST WITH THE SHINY NOSE.

② JEAN-BAPTISTE CARPEAUX WAS A HIGHLY IMPORTANT AND INFLUENTIAL FRENCH SCULPTOR OF BRONZES. HE WAS BORN IN 1827 AND DIED IN 1875.

⑤ THE COLOUR OF THE PATINATION CAN HELP IDENTIFY A PIECE IN THE ABSENCE OF A SIGNATURE. BARYE FAVOURED GREEN.

③ JULES MOIGNIEZ COMMITTED SUICIDE IN 1894. HE CHANGED THE FORM OF HIS SIGNATURE THREE TIMES WHICH HELPS DATE HIS WORK.

⑥ SOME SCULPTORS PAID THE MOST INCREDIBLE ATTENTION TO DETAIL – HERE, THE FRENCH TEXT CAN BE CLEARLY READ.

were signed by the sculptor or marked by the bronze-founder or both. The generally Romantic style of the period is distinctive, and it does not take a great deal of experience to discriminate between, say, a finely detailed animal group modelled and cast by Barye and a later, poorer copy.

POPULAR SUBJECTS

The decorative bronzes of the 19th century were produced in considerable quantity and are fairly readily available in general antique shops today. There are also regular specialist auctions. At the moment Arab subjects of all kinds are popular. Figures mounted on camels are comparatively rare, as are bronzes that incorporate ivory. Any subject involving horses is always much sought after, as is anything faintly risqué. Usually it is the details in the bronze that decide whether it is something out of the ordinary. Of two shying bronze horses of equal quality, for instance, the one which includes a serpent writhing under the fore hooves may fetch more than double the price of the other.

Again, a bronze of a naked girl will command a higher price than one of a young man similarly undressed, and both will cost more than a clothed figure. The presence of a signature on a statue also increases its value considerably.

The Austrian cold-painted bronzes have become extremely popular, and provide a possible area for specialization, as do oriental bronzes or mythological or historical subjects. Animals of all kinds or one particular species would also be a good area for the specialist.

CARE

Bronzes can be displayed in any room in which the humidity is not too high. This means not in bathrooms and conservatories, and not near to windows that are often opened and may admit damp air.

When handling a bronze always pick it up by the main part of the statue and not by an arm or another part that might break off. Check mounted figures to see that the rider is securely attached to the horse. The wearing of cotton gloves will prevent the deposit of corrosive salts from the fingers on to the bronze.

POINTS TO WATCH

■ When cleaning, avoid any polishing. Dust them rather than use solvents or water.
■ Small repairs can be made with epoxy resin adhesive. Badly damaged bronzes should be taken to a metal conservator.

▲ These Chinese bronze geese were used in the mid-18th century as incense burners.

Bedroom Candlesticks

Chambersticks were ideal portable candleholders as they had drip trays to catch the wax, but pairs of candlesticks were used on the dressing table

Candlesticks date back to at least the 10th century. Early ones, especially those used in churches, had a pricket on which the candle was impaled (these are still used in churches). Socket-style candlesticks appeared in the 17th century. Almost all early candlesticks were of metal and were cast in two parts. From about 1750 they were stamped out of sheet metal. Glass and porcelain candlesticks were introduced in the 18th century.

Candles ceased to be the only form of lighting in the Victorian and Edwardian eras as gas and electric lighting were gradually introduced. Gas became popular around the middle of the 19th century, especially in industrial areas, where it was used in factories as well as in homes. Electricity came later, and those who could afford it had electric lighting by the 1880s. As late as 1939, however, only 75 per cent of homes had electricity. Oil lamps also helped oust the candle, though they were never as popular in Britain as they were on the Continent.

Nevertheless, during the Victorian years and well into the 20th century, candles remained a common feature of the household. Candlesticks came in a range of materials, from wood to silver, and in a fantastic jumble of styles, from imitation Jacobean to Art Nouveau. But the commonest form of candlestick used in the Edwardian bedroom was the humble chamberstick, a short-stemmed holder designed for carrying between rooms, and especially useful for lighting the way to bed.

PRACTICAL CHAMBERSTICKS

Chambersticks have remained virtually unchanged from their first appearance in the late 16th century until the 20th century. The risk of fire from flying sparks, or the discomfort of hot wax on the skin made the chamberstick's generous drip tray a vital part of the piece. The tray is usually circular, oval, square or oblong, though it is sometimes octagonal, with a raised lip and a short-stemmed candle sconce in the centre. Early handles were straight, like those of a frying pan, and although this shape persisted, it became less frequent than the flying scroll or loop handle.

Victorian and Edwardian chambersticks usually had a conical extinguisher attached to the handle, and some had a slot in the stem to accommodate a pair of mechanical snuffers. These ingenious instruments, resembling scissors but with a little box on the 'blades', were used to snuff out the

◀ *Two brass snuffer sets, three chambersticks and two brass candlesticks. The tear-shaped snuffer tray and snuffer date from 1750. The snuffer on a rectangular tray with relief edge is an 1840 model. Clockwise from the top, the chambersticks are of brass, enamel and tin. The brass one, of c.1830, has a snuffer hooked on to the handle. The other two are late Victorian. The two candlesticks form an interesting comparison. The one at left, dating from around 1830, has a barley stick stem while the other, of later date, is in a reproduction style.*

▶ *A little unsteady on his feet, this gentleman wisely carries a chamberstick, with its integral drip-tray for the hot wax. Beside him is an old floor-standing candleholder, the height of which can be adjusted by a ratchet.*

▲ *Pretty candlesticks with floral decorations were made to grace a lady's bedroom.*

candle and snip off the burnt wick simultaneously.

Chambersticks were made in vast quantities and their makers and designers are usually unknown. Brass was frequently used, but in Edwardian times chambersticks were also made of pressed glass, Staffordshire earthenware, iron or wood. The simplest ones of all were of enamelled tin, often in pale blue. They cost only a few pence and consisted of a simple circular drip tray with a loop handle big enough for one finger and a crocodile clip soldered to the middle to hold the candle. These were made up until World War I.

Brass chambersticks, with simple handles and trays more like shallow bowls, were also among the cheapest to buy, while elaborately patterned and edged 'Goodnight Candlesticks' in brass could be considerably more expensive. Also available were models with a glass sleeve which fitted over the candle to form a nightlight which would not blow out in a strong draught.

DESIGNER CHAMBERSTICKS

The commonplace nature of chambersticks did not prevent there being more prestigious versions. From 1901 until the 1930s Liberty's produced their pewter Tudric candlesticks and chambersticks. An attractive departure from standard lines, these combined the floral swirls of Art Nouveau with Celtic influences such as concentric curves. Most of

▼ These candlesticks from the 19th and early 20th centuries reveal a wide range of popular materials and styles. Among the six 19th-century candlesticks on the left are examples in brown marble, yellow glass, three cylindrical ones in ceramic and a brass-topped wooden one with a hollow spiral stem. The five at right date from 1900 to the 1920s. At the back of this group is a wooden one painted in green and gold, next to one in bakelite with a brass top. The iridescent pink candlestick is ceramic and the two in front of it are in decorated glass.

these were designed by Archibald Knox, although he was not credited on the pieces. The sticks were made by the Birmingham firm of W. H. Haseler, who were also responsible for Liberty's similar Cymric range in silver.

Silver chambersticks from early in the 19th century, by makers like Matthew Boulton of Birmingham, were treasured, rather than used as everyday household items. Chambersticks did not offer a great opportunity for Victorian elaboration, but silver ones were sometimes made with gadroon borders.

CANDLESTICKS

The chamberstick was not the only candlestick to be found in the bedroom. A useful innovation for the ladies was a pair of very short and squat candlesticks linked by a strap. The strap could be slung over the dressing table mirror so that the candles lit the mirror and the user's face. Dressing table sets, too, included a pair of small candlesticks. These sets comprised a ring tree, jewellery case, trinket box, ointment jar and hatpin holder as well as the candlesticks, and

often came in earthenware, though some were in porcelain. They were made by many of the Staffordshire potteries. Candlesticks became much less common in such sets from about 1900 onwards and complete 20th-century sets are now scarce.

The 19th century saw the production of candlesticks and candelabra in a variety of materials. Elaborate silver and gilded candelabra with fluted Corinthian-style columns were popular. Silver was imitated in silver plate, while more ornate sticks were of Dresden china, and cheaper sticks were made of brass. Baluster designs were popular, in wood or brass. Wooden sticks were also mass produced by machine-turning in the popular barley-sugar twist shape.

There were glass candlesticks with slender plant motifs from the French and Austrian glasshouses, and tall, angular sticks were designed by Charles Rennie Mackintosh. But the dining room was the true home of such candlesticks; the humble chamberstick was the usual bedroom candleholder. It retained its usefulness through the Edwardian years, but as electricity advanced, the chamberstick was forgotten.

Chambersticks, like table sticks, often came in multiples of two, and it is best to attempt to buy pairs.

Check for holes due to excessive polishing of thin 'loaded' silver, and avoid any metal sticks with signs of welding or soldering. Fakes are best detected by experts, but in the case of brass, watch out for modern pieces which have been 'distressed' to age them. Victorian brass is lighter in colour. Silver pieces have sometimes been recast – examine the hallmarks carefully.

◄ *An unusual form of chamberstick, this fine early lamp was fuelled by vegetable oil. The globe amplified the light and protected the flame, and the silver snuff was just like a candle snuff. This rare example dates from 1819, and was designed by Matthew Boulton.*

▲ *A brass chamberstick with an engraved design and a frying pan-style handle. The broad base, which caught the dripping wax and bits of glowing wick, made it safe to carry around the bedroom.*

◄ *An unusual 19th-century candlestick. It is made of a narwhal's tusk mounted in brass, with a decorative brass candleholder.*

BUILDING A COLLECTION

A collection of chambersticks alone might be rather dull; a collection reflecting the great variation in shape, size, style and material of candlesticks is, in general, more interesting. Although candlesticks can be displayed in a case, there is no reason why they should not be kept on display and used.

Both brass and silver should be polished – though not with an abrasive polish – and washed in soapy water from time to time, then wiped with a chamois leather. Wooden sticks should be dusted and occasionally rubbed with a suitable oil – almond oil, for instance. Porcelain candlesticks should be washed with soapy water, as should glass ones.

Look for chambersticks which are undented and unbent, though these are uncommon, since chambersticks got plenty of use and are likely to have been dropped a few times. They are most valuable when complete with original extinguisher and snuffers.

·PRICE GUIDE·

CANDLESTICKS AND CHAMBERSTICKS

Chambersticks may have been more mundane pieces than tablesticks in the first place, but they are now less common – no doubt because they were not kept when electric lighting took over – and are gaining in value. Though the simplest enamel chamberstick from late Victorian or Edwardian times may be purchased for under £10, brass ones are likely to cost nearer £20.

A pair of brass tablesticks will fetch

up to £100. Silver sticks are a different proposition. Fine Victorian and Edwardian silver sticks may fetch hundreds or thousands of pounds – a set of 12 Matthew Boulton silver chambersticks, made in 1803, sold for £28,000 at auction. The Liberty Tudric and Cymric sticks are gaining in value and now fetch hundreds of pounds at auction. Buy pairs where possible – single sticks can be worth as little as an eighth of the value of a pair.

Folding Knives

By the 19th century folding knives combined function with beauty – the finest examples being intricately carved and engraved

A picnic in the last century might have included a surprising array of eating cutlery, some of it designed specifically to be portable. Matching sets comprising a knife, fork, spoon and corkscrew, originally designed for campaigning soldiers, were now ideal for elegant eating on the riverbank in more peaceful times.

THE FIRST FOLDING KNIVES

Folding knives have been traced back to Roman times, when they were used both by the military and civilian population. The folding knife had a multiplicity of uses and its popularity is reflected in the variety of handles cast in bronze or fashioned from bone or ivory. The mechanism was simple – a blade hinged on to a handle slotted to accommodate the blade when it was not in use. There was no spring in the folding knife mechanism at this time.

Mediaeval and Tudor pocket knives still exist but they are rare. This may be due to the fashion of the time of carrying an eating knife in a sheath, which eliminated the need for any other form of personal knife. During the mid-17th century, however, an innovation occurred which resulted in the revival of the folding knife – a spring was added to hold the blade either open or shut.

The convenience and effectiveness of the new folding mechanism was fully exploited during the 18th century. Folding knives were made in many different shapes and sizes according to their requirements. These multi-purpose pocket knives led to the evolution of speciality folding fruit knives, together with other styles for shaping the nibs of quill pens (hence the term 'penknife') and for pruning plants. Veterinarians, fishermen and smokers eventually came to use them as well.

Multi-bladed knives appeared during the early 19th century, some of which attempted to cater for every conceivable need. They ranged from huge exhibition knives like the Norfolk Knife with its 75 tools and blades made by Rodgers for the Great Exhibition, down to miniature models that were less than one inch (25mm) long.

Until the 18th century there were no standard patterns for pocket knives – they had not occupied an important enough niche in social history – but at the end of the 17th

Multi-bladed Knives

THIS 17TH-CENTURY MULTI-BLADED FRENCH FOLDING KNIFE REVEALS THE SKILL OF THE EARLY CUTLERS AND ANTICIPATES THE 19TH-CENTURY CRAZE FOR ALL TYPES OF MULTI-BLADED CREATIONS. THE KNIFE IS 'RIVETLESS' WHICH MEANS THAT THE RIVETS HAVE BEEN DISGUISED BY THE SURROUNDING SILVER OVERLAY DECORATION OF MALE FIGURES AND MYTHICAL BIRDS AND BEASTS. THE DECORATION ALSO EXTENDS TO THE ENGRAVING ON THE SILVER BLADE (WHICH IS PICTURED) AND TO THE SILVER TRIM ALONG THE BACK OF EACH OF THE STEEL BLADES. THERE ARE A NUMBER OF THESE RANGING FROM A SAW TO A SERPETTE USED FOR PRUNING PLANTS.

▶ *A picnic in the park was the ideal opportunity for using personalized and often highly decorative sets of cutlery. Wealthier families, relying as they did on a retinue of servants, could leave the folding, space-saving cutlery behind and take the best china, silver and horn-bladed knives along, no matter how heavy or cumbersome.*

▼ *This exquisite three-piece set is one of the finer examples of travelling cutlery. All three items – knife, spoon and two-pronged fork – are made of silver gilt and mother-of-pearl and come complete with their own shagreen carrying case.*

century they were being modelled in the style of their table cousins.

The blades of table knives were turned up at the end like a scimitar, the tip was rounded and could be used like a spoon for supping sauces, and the handle turned downwards like a pistol butt so that the whole knife was shaped like an elongated letter 'S'. Folding knives soon followed this style. The blade was easy to open since only the cutting edge was enclosed in the haft.

By the 1770s the more typical spear-shaped blade with its sharp point began to appear. To prevent the point from causing injury the blade was now more enclosed in the handle and a nail nick was cut into the blade to facilitate opening. This design for the pocket knife, still used today, first appeared at the turn of the 18th century.

DEFINING THE COMPONENTS

Folding knives have several components and each is made from a variety of materials. The blade is usually made from fine carbon or stainless steel and consists of a cutting edge on the lower side with the 'back' on the upper side. The blade is attached to a centrally pierced square of metal, or tang, which forms the hinge mechanism.

Two sheets of brass or iron, known as webs, are the base plates of the haft or handle and can be seen by looking into the blade slot or along the back of the haft. At the end where the blade is attached the webs are strengthened with a square of extra metal, known as the bolster, to reinforce the knife's fulcrum.

The scales (sometimes called grips) are attached by rivets to the webs and are made from almost any material that is attractive, practicable and durable. Often there is a silver shield set into the handle in which the owner can have his initials engraved. The spring is a hook-shaped piece of spring steel which is pierced in the centre and at the far end, where it curves around the end of the haft, so that it can be riveted in place. The spring exerts pressure on the blade tang and prevents the blade from swinging open.

COMMEMORATIVE KNIVES

After 1900, knives were made as commemoratives, particularly as Coronation souvenirs, and later examples reveal a fashion for souvenirs of popular resorts. Steel-bladed folding knives were made by cutlers while silver-bladed fruit knives were made by silversmiths, some of whom were also cutlers.

During the industrial prosperity of the last century Sheffield steel became world famous with its advances in technology and production. Firms such as Joseph Rogers and George Wostenholm were among the leaders in a host of companies with increasing wealth and power so that the Sheffield cutlers eventually eclipsed their long-standing London rivals.

Decorative Knives

Decorative folding knives were made for followers of fashion or those who could afford something less pedestrian in appearance. French cutlers were among the first to produce silver-bladed folding knives during the later 17th century, and during the next 180 years produced some of the finest decorative folding knives in the world.

Silver blades were used for cutting fruit since they were too soft to be of much other use and – unlike blades of carbon steel – were not stained by fruit acid. As fruit eating was quite a luxury at this time, a fruit knife reflected the owner's social status to a certain degree.

The making of pocket fruit knives started in England during the mid-18th century; they were largely modelled on the French style. Most were made at Sheffield and, during the 19th century, at Birmingham, although the assay offices (where hallmarks are awarded) at London and Chester were occasionally used to assay the many wares of the Sheffield and Birmingham silversmiths.

Individual knives and sets of matching knife and two-tined fork were sold in leather boxes as practical yet attractive gifts. They were deemed suitable for ladies and indeed ladies' names

were often engraved on shields and blades of Victorian examples. Victorian fruit knives demonstrate the change in taste from the classical, elegant lines of the Georgian period to a more florid style of botanical motifs so admired at the time.

Silver blades were often decorated with bright-cut engraving or, later, with trailing vines. The mother-of-pearl hafts were engraved and inlaid with silver wire or carved into designs such as the Prince of Wales' triple plume, a cornucopia or an ear of wheat.

The decorative style of pocket fruit knives also extended to other smaller folding knives such as penknives.

▲ *This tortoiseshell fruit knife has a silver blade and is engraved with the owner's initials.*

PRICE GUIDE ④

◄ *A German fruit knife made of steel and decorated with an enamelled design of autumn oak leaves.*

PRICE GUIDE ③

▲ *Both the mother-of-pearl handle and the silver bolster of this fruit knife are engraved, the bolster shaped like a crown.*

PRICE GUIDE ③

▶ *The mother-of-pearl handle of this silver knife is carved with an image of a crown surmounted by the Prince of Wales feathered plume.*

PRICE GUIDE ④

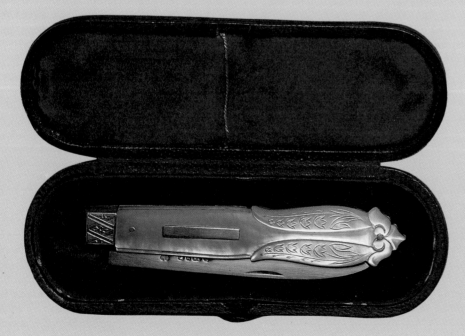

◄ *This fruit knife is scaled with mother-of-pearl of carved snow drop design. It is still in its original lined and hinged box.*

PRICE GUIDE ⑤

PRICE GUIDE

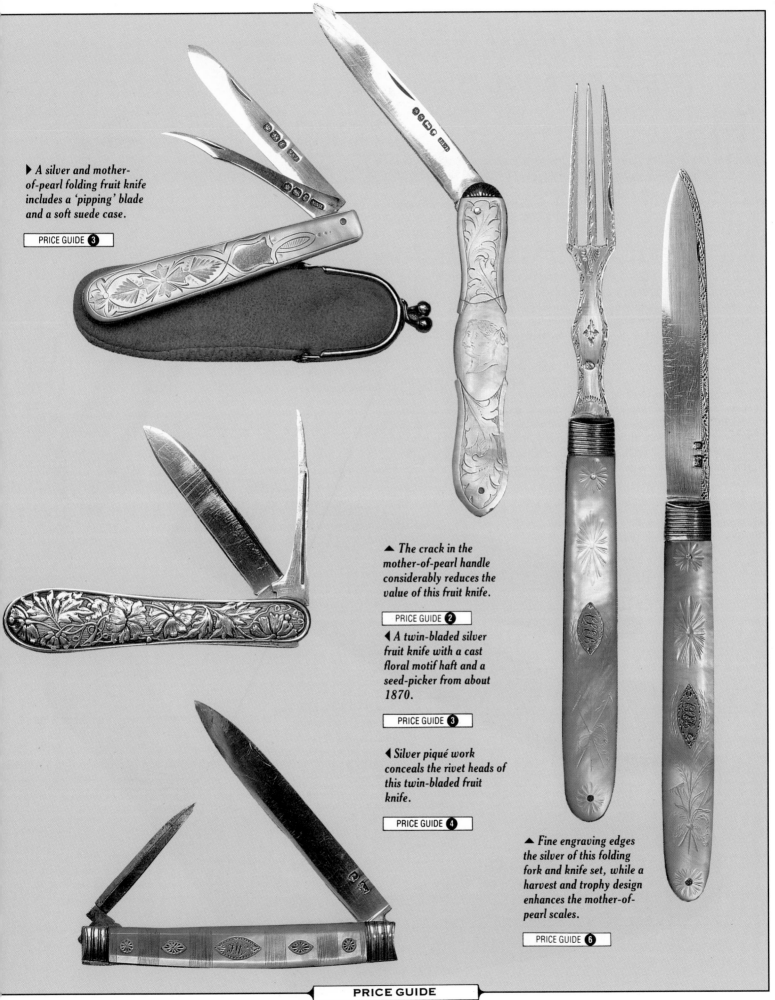

▶ A silver and mother-of-pearl folding fruit knife includes a 'pipping' blade and a soft suede case.

PRICE GUIDE **3**

▲ The crack in the mother-of-pearl handle considerably reduces the value of this fruit knife.

PRICE GUIDE **2**

◀ A twin-bladed silver fruit knife with a cast floral motif haft and a seed-picker from about 1870.

PRICE GUIDE **3**

◀ Silver piqué work conceals the rivet heads of this twin-bladed fruit knife.

PRICE GUIDE **4**

▲ Fine engraving edges the silver of this folding fork and knife set, while a harvest and trophy design enhances the mother-of-pearl scales.

PRICE GUIDE **6**

PRICE GUIDE

Functional Folding Knives

However exotic decorative folding knives became, their plainer cousins were used more often and, because they were kept carefully, have generally survived just as well.

The earliest examples to be found in the antique trade tend to date from the later 18th century and have characteristic pistol-grip hafts. Some of these were hafted with brass cast with contemporary exaltations for King George III or warnings of the blade's sharpness. Over 100 years later folding knives were used by nearly everyone and their multiplicity of purpose is reflected in the number of tools that were built into them.

Most of these knives have a rather masculine feel about them – quite heavy and built to last. The blades and springs of some

were slightly decorated with filework. Folding knives for women exist and a few sets were made as 'his and hers'. In the 19th century there were also a number of novelty knives made in such shapes as women's legs or geisha girls.

Purely utilitarian pocket fruit knives are recognizable by their thin, whippy blades made of silver or of silverplated 'German silver' (cupro-nickel), and plain mother-of-pearl scales.

Haft scales show an amazing diversity of materials that were, and still are, used – various woods, horn and bone, sometimes 'jiggered' to resemble staghorn. By the late 19th century, plastics such as ivorine, complete with the markings found in ivory, and xylo, which resembles dark wood, were also commonplace.

▶ *A miniature folding sewing knife has an ivory handle, in the shape of a Japanese lady, and three silver blades.*

PRICE GUIDE ❺

▶ *The unusual ivory handle of this double-bladed quill knife is in the form of a cloaked woman holding a partridge.*

PRICE GUIDE ❹

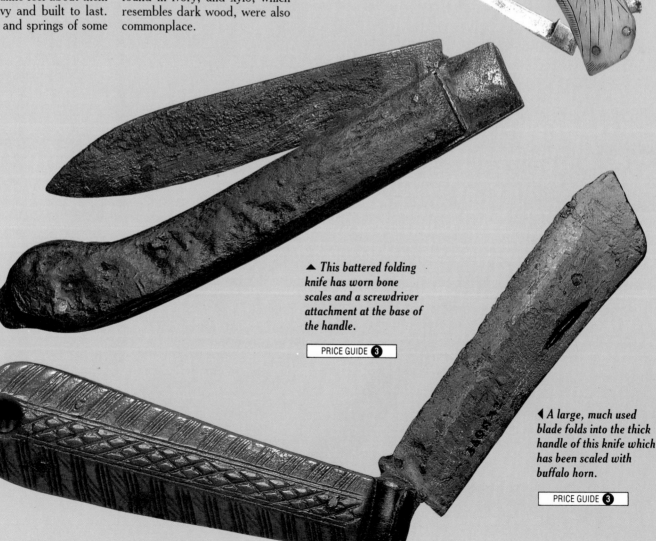

▲ *This battered folding knife has worn bone scales and a screwdriver attachment at the base of the handle.*

PRICE GUIDE ❸

◀ *A large, much used blade folds into the thick handle of this knife which has been scaled with buffalo horn.*

PRICE GUIDE ❸

◀ *The long bolster on this large folding knife is a characteristic of the 'Barlow' style.*

PRICE GUIDE ❸

▲ *Said to be modelled on Lady Ilchester's leg, this novelty knife was made by the firm of Neesham c. 1870.*

PRICE GUIDE ❸

▲ *A cross-hatch design adorns the dark bone scales of this bulky pocket knife.*

PRICE GUIDE ❸

▼ *The blade of this early penknife has broken off but the bone spike, used for splitting quills, is intact.*

PRICE GUIDE ❸

◀ *This French souvenir knife from Aix les Bains is made of horn and inlaid with silver and local shell fragments.*

PRICE GUIDE ❸

COLLECTOR'S TIPS

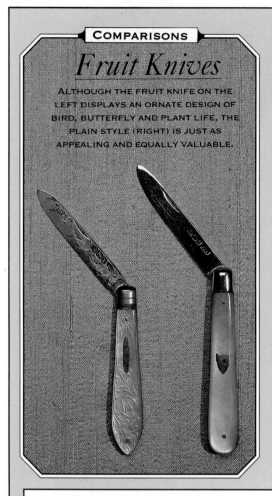

COMPARISONS

Fruit Knives

ALTHOUGH THE FRUIT KNIFE ON THE LEFT DISPLAYS AN ORNATE DESIGN OF BIRD, BUTTERFLY AND PLANT LIFE, THE PLAIN STYLE (RIGHT) IS JUST AS APPEALING AND EQUALLY VALUABLE.

A recent upsurge of interest shown by the antique trade in folding knives, as their collectability has been realised, has resulted in poorer quality items reaching the market. Some, which are not 'quite right' or which are worn out, are still offered for sale at prices that do not reflect their condition. There are many pointers, some quite subtle, which can show whether or not a folding knife has been altered.

VALUABLE FEATURES
The value of a folding knife depends both on the crispness of its mechanism and on its overall appearance. More decorative examples, or those with precious metal blades, are obviously more desirable to collectors than plainer or utilitarian knives. The presence of more blades or tools increases the value, but check for breakages.

Desirable features include gold blades (which were unhallmarked on Sheffield-made pieces until 1904); finely inlaid scales and engraved blades; and interesting inscriptions. On Victorian or later pieces there is often finely carved mother-of-pearl. Look particularly for knives made by Aaron Hadfield between 1820 and 1840 or by J. Y. Cowlishaw between 1840 and 1880. Their carved hafts often show more

imagination and skill than those of other craftsmen. After 1880, however, Cowlishaw's workshop started to turn out more mass-produced items. Knives in their original boxes, particularly ornate ones, are highly sought after by collectors.

SILVER HALLMARKS
A variety of hallmarks are often found on silver blades. Before 1820 only two or three hallmarks were struck on the blade, with the rest placed on the tang so as not to clutter the blade. After 1820 a slight reduction in hallmark size enabled all the marks to be struck on the blade. Examples of these hallmarks include: the assay office (e.g. crown for Sheffield, anchor for Birmingham); sterling quality (lion passant); duty (monarch's head); date letter (year of assay); and the maker's marks.

CHECKING FOR DEFECTS
Anyone thinking about buying a folding knife should be aware of the different types of defects which can affect the value. Some of these defects involve the decoration of the handle, although most concern the blade and the mechanism which allows it to fold.

Make sure that the blade is original. It is not too difficult to replace one blade with

A Soldier's Set

THIS SET, KNOWN AS A COMPANION SET, CONSISTS OF THREE FOLDING PIECES — A KNIFE, A FORK AND A LARGE SPOON INCLUDING A CORKSCREW. EACH PIECE HAS A BONE HANDLE ENGRAVED WITH AN INSCRIPTION AND AN ILLUSTRATION. THE ENGRAVING AND THE WRITING ON THE BASE OF THE CARRYING CASE (NOT SHOWN) PUT TOGETHER A STORY OF A 'FINE OLD SOLDIER' (MAJOR FREDERICK JAMES TAYLOR OF THE 10TH NORTH LINCOLNSHIRE REGIMENT) WHO USED THIS SET ON ACTIVE DUTY. THE SET WAS PROBABLY GIVEN TO THE MAJOR ON HIS 40TH BIRTHDAY, SINCE HE WAS BORN IN 1846, AND PASSED DOWN IN THE FAMILY FINALLY GOING 'TO DAVID FROM UNCLE FRANK' IN 1943.

① BOTH THE HALLMARKS ON THE BACK OF THE FORK AND THE NAME STAMPED ON THE FRONT OF THE KNIFE INDICATE THAT THE SET WAS MADE BY JOSEPH MAPPIN OF SHEFFIELD.

② ALL THREE OF THE BONE HANDLES HAVE BEEN ENGRAVED WITH THE MAJOR'S NAME, HIS REGIMENT AND THE DATE HE WAS PRESENTED WITH THE SET.

③ THE CUTLERY SHOWS SIGNS OF WEAR.

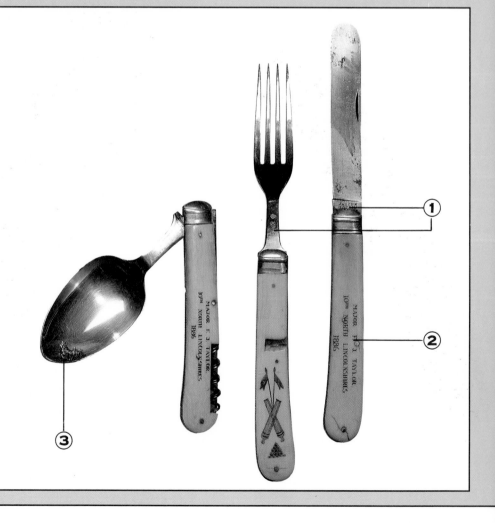

·CLOSE UP·

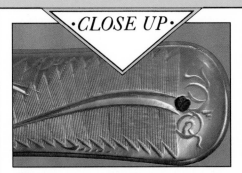

① ENGRAVED MOTHER-OF-PEARL

② INITIALLED PLATE

③ MINIATURE KNIFE

④ CONCEALED RIVET

⑤ SILVER HANDLE

⑥ HALLMARKS

① A FINE QUILL PATTERN HAS BEEN ENGRAVED ON TO A MOTHER-OF-PEARL HANDLE.

④ THE RIVET HAS BEEN CLEVERLY DISGUISED AS THE CENTRE OF AN ETCHED FLOWER.

② THE OWNER'S INITIALS HAVE BEEN CAREFULLY CUT INTO THE METAL SHIELD OF THIS FRUIT KNIFE.

⑤ THE HAFT OF THIS FRUIT KNIFE HAS BEEN SCALED WITH AN ENGRAVED SILVER FLORAL DESIGN.

③ THIS MINIATURE FOLDING SEWING KNIFE CONSISTS OF THREE TINY SILVER BLADES.

⑥ THE HALLMARKS STRUCK ON THE SILVER BLADE INCLUDE THE ASSAY AND CROWN MARKS.

another. The hinge pin should blend in with the bolster decoration. The mechanism may feel clumsy or the hallmarks (if silver) may show that the blade is later than the decorative style of the handle.

The blade should reach to the end of the blade slot. If not, the tip has probably been broken off and the broken end filed back to the appropriate shape.

If the blade refuses to close into the handle and remains partly sprung out, this indicates that the corners of the tang have worn away. The blade may flop about unless the sides of the bolster have been squeezed in a vice to prevent this. Avoid knives with this fault as they are difficult to repair. Inspect the shut knife at the blade end to assess wear to the tang. This type of fault is usually common to knives made post-1870 when springs were cut by machine ('blanked') and were consequently thicker and less effective than previously.

The blade should open and close freely without either stiffness or looseness. The spring should rise and fall; if it does not, this could mean that either the tang is worn, that the spring is strained or cracked or that the balance rivet, securing the centre of the spring, has worked loose from the handle.

Repaired blades can be detected by partly-melted hallmarks or lumpy areas of solder, usually near the tang. Multi-bladed penknives were made as forerunners of disposable-bladed knives – when one blade broke another could be used instead – therefore check that the cutler's mark, found on the tang, corresponds to all the blades.

Some of the more obvious faults of antique folding knives are cracked scales; sometimes the dealer's price label is carefully (and shamefully) stuck over a crack. Mother-of-pearl scales may also be chipped or heated (dry and brown looking) which will halve the value.

Replaced scales are harder to detect but look for an obvious disparity in the texture, not necessarily the colour, of the scales on each side of the knife.

CARING FOR FOLDING KNIVES
Folding knives are easy to care for but may require the following treatment. Oil the mechanism if it is at all stiff; this is most important and will dramatically increase the knife's life. Tortoiseshell scales may require some natural oil, such as almond oil, to be rubbed in; this will enhance the appearance of dry scales. Rusty blades can be cleaned up with fine wire wool and penetrating oil, then polished with a soft paper.

POINTS TO WATCH
■ Decorative and multi-bladed knives are more valuable than plainer examples.
■ Blades should fit properly into the handle and the spring mechanism should produce a crisp movement.
■ Silver blades will bear hallmarks and maker's marks indicating the date and place of manufacture.

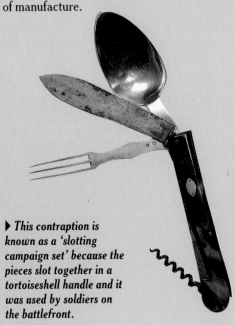

▶ *This contraption is known as a 'slotting campaign set' because the pieces slot together in a tortoiseshell handle and it was used by soldiers on the battlefront.*

The Fender

The Victorian hearth was instantly eye-catching – not just for its captivating flames but also for its shiny bright fender and fire-irons in well-polished steel or brass

To Victorians, the heart of a room was its fireplace: traditionally capacious, ornate and radiating cheer. In the drawing room of a country house it would dominate an entire wall, the flamboyant marble surround setting off a gleaming grate and fender. Such a fireplace formed a compelling focus and the room's very activity centred on it, although partly through necessity. While the fire sent out a scorching heat, it only affected the immediate vicinity and the greater part of the room remained uncomfortably chilly, plagued by numbing draughts that whistled across to the chimney from ill-fitting windows and doors. Thus the family and their guests gravitated towards the hearth. For gentlemen the warmest, and therefore most prized, position was leaning languorously against the mantelshelf; for ladies, it was sitting on the fender bench.

THE ROLE OF THE FENDER

Fenders properly became part of the English fireplace in the 17th century – thanks to the increasing use of sea-coal (so called because it was transported from mining areas in the north-east by boat). The new fuel burnt differently from wood. Instead of lying on a wide open hearth, it had to be kept together and also required good ventilation. As a result, fire openings were made smaller and fitted with a raised grate, or basket, which both held the coals and provided adequate draught underneath. Although efficient, grates had one hazardous habit; red-hot cinders and sparks would drop out and scatter into the room. It was to contain this wayward ash that fenders were introduced. In the country, however, wood was still the popular fuel, where it remained in favour while coal flourished in the city. And although fenders may have been designed to contain coal cinders, they also proved quite useful in containing the sparks and burning logs thrown out by spitting wood fires.

When first introduced, fenders were set straight across the fire opening but since as many embers fell in front as behind, they were then either pulled out in a serpentine shape or brought forward and, in the mid-1700s, given corners, thus forming a rectangular curb. The side return sections were often specifically shaped as supports for fire-irons.

FENDER STYLES

Early fenders generally consisted of brass or copper sheets on an iron base. Inevitably, they followed fireplace fashion in both materials and decoration, and by Victorian times were predominately of steel or brass. Cast iron was also a popular material, especially for smaller or more humble rooms. But in the grandeur of a country drawing room, with its lavish dimensions and opulent furnishings and where the fireplace, in magnificent marble, dominated, the fender was almost certainly crafted in the same marble or in gleaming steel (polished daily by the maid with rotten-stone, a metal-cleaning powder, and sweet oil, commonly olive oil).

Fender decoration took many forms. Metal was often embossed, engraved or pierced, producing a wide array of shapes and styles to choose from. The more elaborate fenders frequently featured foliage motifs, animal designs, scrollwork or geometric patterns, some with crenellated tops and sculpted feet as an additional decoration.

On a more practical level, some fenders included a

▼ No Victorian country or town house was complete without a fireplace. As the room's main attraction, much attention was paid to its appearance as well as to the many accessories needed to keep it in good working order.

trivet for warming the hot-water jug while many stood 12-14 inches (30-35 cm) tall – high enough to prevent long dresses, especially full-skirted crinolines, from sweeping into the fire. Towards the end of the 19th century, two types of tall fender incorporated seating. One, the club fender, featured a full-length bench seat. The other, the seat curb, had two box seats; padded lids opened to reveal a coal box with a lift-out metal container at one end and storage for slippers at the other.

HEARTH FURNISHINGS

In addition to the fender, hearth furnishings included fire-irons, firedogs and other accessories. Many of the grand country houses may have used coal as a convenient substitute for wood from time to time. Because of this, the Victorian drawing room would have contained a large collection of hearth furnishings to accommodate both types of fuel. When wood predominated, the most common fire-tool was a two-pronged fork, about 4 feet (1.2 metres) long, which served to push logs back into the embers. The changeover to coal, however, necessitated different equipment. Tongs and a shovel were used for putting lumps onto the fire and a poker for stirring them. These new-style fire-irons first made their appearance in the 18th century. Early models were of iron or steel and, since fireplaces were still relatively large, up to 3 feet (1 metre) long. By Victorian times, fire openings had shrunk and irons became correspondingly shorter, around 18 to 20 inches (45-50 cm) in length, although larger ones were still made for use in grand fireplaces such as might grace a country drawing room.

The set, which now included a brush for sweeping up ash, often matched the fender and other fire furniture. During the first half of the 19th century, polished steel was in vogue, but from the 1850s brass predominated. The shaft, often reeded, fluted or twisted, fitted into a handle which was itself fretted, embossed, engraved, and embellished with twirls. Ornamental knobs were turned or cast in designs like the head of Queen Victoria or a fleur-de-lis. Further

decoration appeared on the shovel pan, which was frequently fretted, and on the hinge of the tongs. Victorian tongs tended to have claw feet as opposed to the disc terminals of the previous century.

Fire-iron sets, particularly shorter models, generally had matching holders which stood just inside or outside the fender, depending on the space available. Some sets incorporated a second pair of tongs known as ember tongs: these were used to extract a glowing coal from the grate to light a pipe or, indeed, another fire. Although seldom included in a companion hearth set, bellows used for encouraging a sluggish fire were equally ornate, with embellishment on the metal nozzle and handle. Decorative studs securing the leather and carved or inlaid designs on the wooden sides added to the design.

Alongside the other accessories, a well-equipped

▲ The expansive layout of many Victorian houses meant that the warming atmosphere of a fireplace was appreciated at any time of the day. The gentleman of the house's favourite spot might have been right by the fire, leaning against the mantelshelf.

Fender Styles

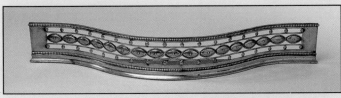

THIS SERPENTINE-SHAPED FENDER IS IN POLISHED STEEL. THE METAL WAS OFTEN EMBOSSED, ENGRAVED OR PIERCED TO PRODUCE INTRICATE PATTERNS.

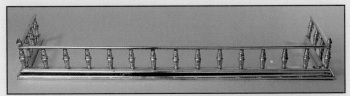

ALONG WITH STEEL AND CAST IRON, BRASS WAS A POPULAR MATERIAL FOR VICTORIAN FENDERS. THIS BRASS BOBBIN FENDER IS DATED 1880.

RUNNING THE FULL LENGTH OF THE HEARTH, CLUB FENDERS WERE NORMALLY MADE OF BRASS OR STEEL WITH AN UPHOLSTERED LEATHER TOP SERVING AS A BENCH.

The Chimney Sweep

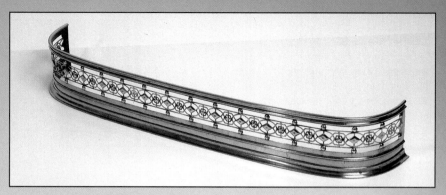

IN VICTORIAN TIMES A LARGE HOUSE, WITH FIRES BURN-
ING DAILY IN MANY DIFFERENT ROOMS, WOULD HAVE ITS
CHIMNEY SWEPT FOUR OR FIVE TIMES A YEAR; AND EACH
SWEEPING MIGHT PRODUCE AS MUCH AS TWO BUSHELS OF
SOOT WHICH SPREAD INTO THE ROOM, COVERING EVERY
SURFACE IN GREASY BLACK DUST. CLEARING UP AFTER
THE SWEEP'S VISIT WAS ONE OF THE MAID'S WORST TASKS.

GETTING AT THE SOOT INSIDE THE NARROW CHIMNEY WAS
EQUALLY TROUBLESOME AND SO, FROM THE EARLY
1800S, MANY SWEEPS EMPLOYED SMALL BOYS, AS
YOUNG AS FIVE OR SIX, TO CLEAN CHIMNEYS BY CLIMBING
THEM. SCALING AN OPENING, PERHAPS ONLY 10 INCHES
(25CM) WIDE, OFTEN CAUSED BRUISING AND SCRATCHING
AND THE EYES AND LUNGS BECAME FILLED WITH SOOT.
EVEN WORSE, CLIMBERS FREQUENTLY GOT WEDGED AND
OFTEN DIED BEFORE THEY COULD BE RESCUED. THE SCAN-
DAL OF BOY SWEEPS WAS FORCEFULLY HIGHLIGHTED BY
CHARLES KINGSLEY IN *THE WATER BABIES* (1863) AND
THEIR USE WAS FINALLY BANNED BY AN ACT OF PARLIA-
MENT IN 1875.

▲ *Polished steel fenders
were a popular choice to
accompany Victorian
marble fireplaces. The
gleaming effect was
achieved by frequently
polishing the metal.*

PRICE GUIDE ❺

▶ *Although most of the
items surrounding the
fireplace served a specific
purpose, these brass
pheasants simply added a
touch of elegance.*

PRICE GUIDE ❹

▼ *This free-standing fire guard is made of steel mesh topped
by a shining brass rail and dates to the later half of the
18th century.*

PRICE GUIDE ❺

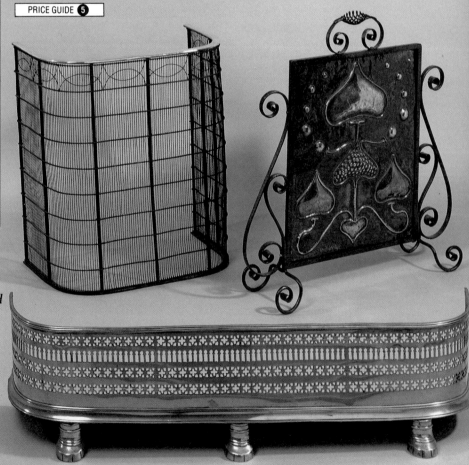

▶ *This 1900s Arts &
Crafts screen rests on
beautifully turned cast-iron
legs. The screen itself is
made of copper with a
raised motif.*

PRICE GUIDE ❹

▶ *This finely pierced,
polished brass fender, dated
1780, is conventionally
curved but, more
unusually, is raised on
three legs.*

PRICE GUIDE ❻

collection may have also included a few gadgets, such as a toasting fork or a chestnut roaster for making fireside snacks.

The wood-burning fireplace included a pair of andirons or a log basket. Andirons – also known as firedogs – have tall upright shafts standing on short sturdy front legs, and long back legs. Logs were rested across the back legs behind the shafts which prevented the logs from rolling out of the fire. Log baskets were often built in to the fire opening, usually by being attached to the back of the hearth.

BASKETS, SCUTTLES AND BOXES

The advent of coal also gave birth to special containers for carrying and storage. Initially, coal was brought into the house in buckets and kept beside the fire in baskets. However, as grimy coal dust seeped through the open wickerwork all too easily, baskets soon gave way to solid-sided scuttles and boxes.

Like other fire equipment, scuttles were decorated, especially if they were used for storing coal beside the fireplace rather than just bringing it up from the cellar. In well-to-do households, however,

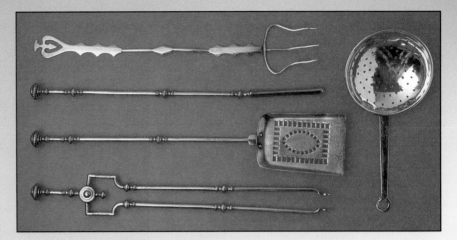

scuttles primarily served for carrying coal. When summoned, servants would bring coal in to replenish the fire, then take the scuttle out again. Nevertheless, even in the wealthiest home, a small supply of coal would also be stored beside the hearth, either in a coal box or coal vase.

Boxes, in mahogany, oak or walnut, featured either drop-fronts or lift-up lids and usually came in pairs – one for each side of the fire. Inside, they had a detachable metal container for the coal. Outside, the boxes glistened with copper or brass ornament. For use in main reception rooms, boxes were often of metal, japanned black with painted floral decoration, or they were supplanted by coal vases – tall, elegant metal receptacles.

▲ *Alongside the fender, hearth accessories included brass chestnut roasters and copper toasting forks, as well as various fire-irons, such as a steel poker, shovel and tongs.*

FENDERS & FIRE-IRONS

The recent revival of the open fireplace has generated a great demand for hearth furnishings and accessories. Most well-stocked antique shops carry fairly expensive items, although bargains can still be found.

▼ *Although andirons or firedogs were originally used as supports for roasting spits, they soon developed the long back legs capable of supporting large logs.*

PRICE GUIDE 6

▼ *Over the centuries, andirons became ornamental, with the stress on the upright, tall shafts which could be highly decorative like these steel examples dated c. 1860.*

PRICE GUIDE 7

▲ *A steel fire grate with ornate side supports and pierced steel band across the front. Fine pieces such as this, in good condition, fetch high prices.*

PRICE GUIDE 7

◀ *This bow-shaped, Regency steel fender is in the elegant, neo-classical style typical of the period. It is dated 1820.*

PRICE GUIDE 6

Warming Pans

Victorian beds were warmed with a variety of items – metal warming pans, earthenware 'pigs' and rubber hot-water bottles like those still used today

Comfort and etiquette were essential features of Victorian middle-class social life. Mrs Beeton and other writers gave precise instructions to hostesses as to how to offer hospitality to their guests. And it would be a serious breach of conduct not to pay full attention to visitors' needs – not least of which was a comfortable night's sleep after the rigours of travel. In a cold, damp climate such as Edinburgh's, this would involve making sure that the bed-sheets of the guest room were thoroughly aired with a metal warming pan filled with either hot embers or hot water.

EARLY DESIGNS

Although the warming pan might seem typically Victorian in its evocation of cosy home comforts, its origins are much earlier. Warming pans had been used in England since the 16th century, and in Europe from a century earlier – superseding the old method of sending a servant in advance to warm up the bed for the master. At first they were reserved for those of a sickly disposition or for women nearing labour, but in the 17th century they came into more general use among the richer classes. Although a good number of 17th-century pans can be found in antique shops, most warming pans that come on the market date from 1720 onwards.

From the earliest examples until those of the Victorian era, the design of the warming pan remained essentially the same – a long-handled metal pan, with a hinged, pierced lid that fitted over the hot charcoals with which the pan was filled. It would be carried into the bedroom and moved between the bed sheets until the bed was aired and warm. Less efficient servants might leave the pan in place for too long – household accounts indicate that a great many beds were destroyed by fire.

Once it had served its purpose, the warming pan would be returned to the kitchen, emptied, and hung on a hook near the fireplace by means of a ring attached to the end of the handle. The decorative effect of the wall-hung warming pan led to a revival of its popularity in the 1970s and '80s – as a collectable ornament rather than a functional utensil. The reproduction ornamental warming pans readily available today are much less substantial than the real thing – the metal is thinner. They also usually lack the ornate piercing and hammered decorations of the functional originals.

The design of the warming pan was modified over the centuries. Sizes became progressively smaller: 17th-century pans are usually 12-15 inches (30-38 cm) in diameter and have a relatively deep bowl, while those made after 1750 are smaller and shallower. Shapes changed a little too – early examples generally have flat lids and straight sides, while from the 18th century onwards, domed lids and curved sides were favoured.

The main change, however, was in the choice of materials. Early warming pans were made of iron, but by the 16th century brass and, more rarely, copper were used. The handles – which were up to 3 feet (1 metre) long – were initially made of cast or wrought iron, and then of solid cast brass. Metal

▲ The traveller visiting friends or relations in the country would be greeted with a cup of tea. The kettle sat on the coals and later in the evening, after supper, these same coals would be placed in the warming pan that hung on the wall nearby. In the towns, more go-ahead people would have had water-filled warming pans by the beginning of the 19th century.

Changing Styles

THE EARLIEST WARMING PANS WERE COAL-FILLED AND HAD HOLES IN THE LID WHICH LET OXYGEN IN TO KEEP THE COALS ALIGHT.

WATER-FILLED WARMING PANS — THIS ONE IS OF COPPER — HAD NO HOLES AND A STOPPER FOR FILLING. THERE WAS NO RISK OF FIRE.

THE WATER-FILLED EARTHENWARE 'PIG' WAS MORE VERSATILE AND COULD BE LEFT IN THE BED TO WARM THE FEET.

▶ An early Dutch warming pan made wholely of brass. The inscription dates the pan to 1602 and, translated, it reads: 'This pan is suited for women who like to sleep in a warm bed and who have nobody to warm them, so that they have to fire their bed by means of a pan if they haven't got a man who can warm their feet for them.' Venus and Cupid are the central figures.

▲ *This illustration from* Life in London, *published in 1821, shows a maid heating the master's four-poster with a warming pan. The long handle makes this operation easier. The engraving is by Robert and George Cruikshank.*

copper warming pans were produced in great numbers. Silver warming pans from the 17th and early 18th century can occasionally be found, but they are extremely rare.

FUNCTIONAL ORNAMENT
The lid of a warming pan was pierced in order to allow the heat to escape, and piercing became ornamental as well as practical. Some very pretty designs can be found. In the early 1600s the lid was ornamented with both relief patterns and a series of small holes arranged in a circle. From the mid-17th century the piercing became increasingly complex, and resembled elaborate lacework or coarse filigree. The owner's coat of arms was a popular motif around this time. Ornamental brass warming pans became a popular choice of wedding present, and many 17th-century examples bear the initials of the bridal couple and the date of the ceremony.

The Dutch craftsmen who had settled in Britain in the 17th century led the way in design on copper pans – producing fine traceries in shallow engraving. Star shapes, flowers and foliage executed in a series of fine dots were popular. Hammered relief patterns were also common – sometimes depicting complex scenes such as figures set in a landscape.

handles would have been exceedingly hot to hold and added to the already substantial weight of the filled pan, so they were gradually replaced by handles made of wood. Both metal and wooden handles were attractively shaped, with decorative swellings known as 'knops', sometimes with additional brass finials, and an ornate metal plate where the handle was fixed to the pan. Beech, oak, box, ebony, ash and other hardwoods were used for the wooden handles.

Copper was rarely used in the manufacture of warming pans before the 18th century, since impurities caused the metal to crack – potentially hazardous if the pan fractured when filled with hot coals. But in 1728, John Cook perfected a method of machine-rolling copper into workable sheets and

HOT-WATER BOTTLES
Towards the end of the 18th century, water-filled warming pans came into vogue. When water replaced hot charcoal as a source of heat, the traditional basic shape was retained, but the pans generally lacked the ornamentation of the coal-heated

PIGS AND WARMING PANS

Reproduction warming pans are lighter, shinier and often not as well made as the genuine article. The style of rivetting is a good guide to age. A replacement newish, handle does not necessarily devalue an old pan.

◄ *A two-tone earthenware hot-water bottle made by the Langley Pottery in the late 19th century.*

PRICE GUIDE ❸

▲ *A late Victorian copper warming pan with a stained beech handle.*

PRICE GUIDE ❹

▶ *A copper warming pan with a brass lid. It dates from around 1835.*

PRICE GUIDE ❺

versions. The pan was made watertight by means of a screw stopper set either at the side, or in the centre of the upper surface. By the 19th century, warming-pan handles had become detachable, and after 1820, they were often disposed of altogether. This style of water-filled metal warming pan remained popular until the manufacture of earthenware hot-water bottles.

These earthenware bottles were affectionately known as 'pigs'. They were mostly plain, but some were highly decorated with blue and white tinglazing or were made of scratchware – with designs incised on them before firing. The relatively plain examples were usually of cylindrical shape, with a flattened bottom, or were a flattened oval. More fancy designs included those shaped like Gladstone bags – Royal Doulton even produced bottles shaped like bears and dogs. Often 'pigs' are marked with the manufacturer's name and/or trademark.

Hot-water bottles were also made in copper, with attractive brass stoppers. They were either cylindrical (with or without ribbing), or were circular, with flat bottoms. They had to be covered in knitted or embroidered fabric 'coats' to prevent scorching since, unlike hot ember pans, they were left in the bed.

These copper 'bed warmers', as they were known, never achieved the same popularity as the 'pig', and nothing like that of the moulded rubber hot-water bottle which became the main alternative to the earthenware 'pig' from the 1890s onwards. The rubber hot-water bottle is still the most common bedwarmer today – and surprisingly, unlike the wall-hanging warming pan, it is a Victorian invention.

Warming Devices

PORTABLE WARMING DEVICES WERE BIG BUSINESS AND WERE NOT CONFINED TO THE BEDROOM. FOOT WARMERS (BELOW) MIGHT BE USED IN THE BED BUT THEY WERE ALSO IDEAL FOR THE PARLOUR, AND THERE WERE SPECIAL CARRIAGE FOOT WARMERS FOR THOSE CHILLY DRIVES. STOMACH WARMERS (BOTTOM RIGHT) WERE CURVED TO FIT AND WERE SUITABLE FOR THE INFIRM. HAND WARMERS (LEFT) COULD BE KEPT IN A MUFF OR CARRIED IN A POCKET. THE BED AIRER (BOTTOM LEFT) IS, LIKE MOST OF THESE DEVICES, DESIGNED TO BE FILLED WITH HOT WATER.

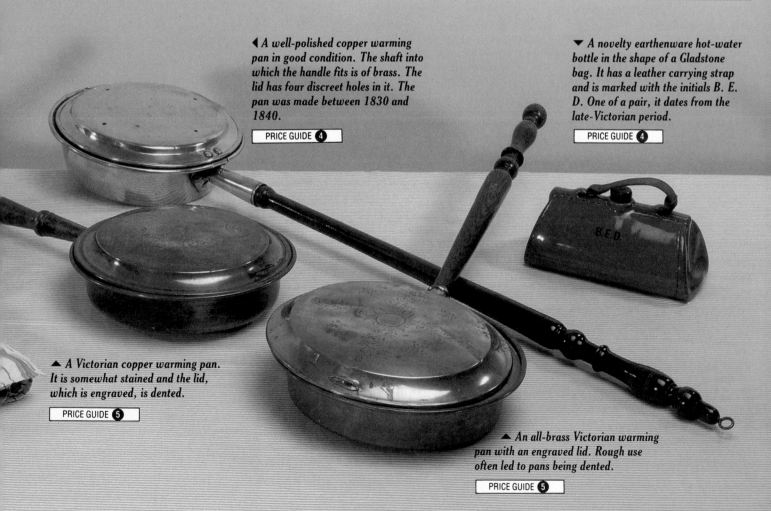

◀ *A well-polished copper warming pan in good condition. The shaft into which the handle fits is of brass. The lid has four discreet holes in it. The pan was made between 1830 and 1840.*

PRICE GUIDE **4**

▼ *A novelty earthenware hot-water bottle in the shape of a Gladstone bag. It has a leather carrying strap and is marked with the initials B. E. D. One of a pair, it dates from the late-Victorian period.*

PRICE GUIDE **4**

▲ *A Victorian copper warming pan. It is somewhat stained and the lid, which is engraved, is dented.*

PRICE GUIDE **5**

▲ *An all-brass Victorian warming pan with an engraved lid. Rough use often led to pans being dented.*

PRICE GUIDE **5**

Art Metalware

Arts and Crafts designers produced functional but artistic wares
in copper and brass, while elaborate art nouveau pieces were
being wrought in pewter and silver

The decades around the turn of the century were a period of great innovation in art metalwork. Two main design strands are clearly discernible. One was the straight-line, avant-garde style, with functionalism as its keynote, which was the product of the Arts and Crafts Movement in Britain. The other was the curvilinear extravagance of a new style, first called Anglo-French and later Art Nouveau, which originated in France.

ARTS AND CRAFTS
William Morris, founder of the Arts and Crafts Movement, in violent reaction to the Victorian taste for over-decoration, believed that form should be dictated by function. When the young William Benson came to consult him about a career, Morris steered him towards metalware. The domestic objects that W. A. S. Benson produced in his factory in Hammersmith – jugs and lamps, kettles and teapots, firescreens and trays, even thermos flasks – were hugely influential and typify the Arts and Crafts aesthetic. They were well-made, simple, practical and elegant in design, and – importantly – were relatively cheap. This was partly because of the materials that Benson used – inexpensive copper and brass had previously only been used below stairs – and partly because of his methods of mass production.

Among craftsmen, Benson was almost alone in his use of mass production. One of

the basic tenets of the Arts and Crafts Movement was the supremacy of the hand-crafted over the factory-made. Typical of the period were the Guilds and small workshops that were set up all over the country to produce art metalware. Among these were the Century Guild founded by A. H. Mackmurdo, the Macdonald sisters' studio in Glasgow, the Newlyn Class in Cornwall, the Silver Studio which concentrated on designs, the Guild of Handicraft and the Birmingham Guild of Handicraft whose motto was 'By hammer and hand'. One of the disappointments of these designers was that their hand-crafted work remained too expensive for most pockets.

The Arts and Crafts Movement rescued silver manufacture from the low ebb that the big firms had brought it to in the late 19th century. C. R. Ashbee, one of the foremost of the new designers in silver and silver-plated wares, founded the Guild and School of Handicraft in 1888. To Ashbee the factory finish was anathema, and he encouraged his silversmiths to leave hammer marks clearly visible on the finished articles.

The first metalwork instructor at the Guild of Handicraft was John Pearson who was eventually dismissed by Ashbee for also supplying Morris & Co. with his embossed metal dishes. Pearson became a master of repoussé work – metalwork designs hammered in low-relief – and his sea-serpents, peacocks, galleons and stylized flowers were distinctive motifs, used to adorn plates and

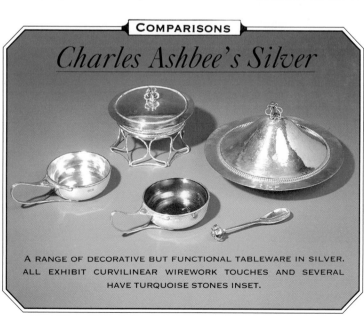

COMPARISONS

Charles Ashbee's Silver

A RANGE OF DECORATIVE BUT FUNCTIONAL TABLEWARE IN SILVER.
ALL EXHIBIT CURVILINEAR WIREWORK TOUCHES AND SEVERAL
HAVE TURQUOISE STONES INSET.

▶ *Three very typical pieces of pewter from WMF, the noted German manufacturer. All were made around the turn of the century. The mirror frame, particularly, exhibits the swirling curvilinear lines for which WMF was known. The candelabrum is one of a valuable and attractive pair.*

▲ *Metalworkers of C. R. Ashbee's Guild of Handicraft in about 1901. None of the techniques of mass production was used here – each worker is making a different piece. The craftsman in the foreground is finishing a bowl with a hammer. The workers took pride in the fact that the marks of hand workmanship were visible on the finished object.*

dishes as well as the copper panels in furniture that were a feature of the time.

ART NOUVEAU

The influence of Art Nouveau is clearly visible in much of Ashbee's more elaborate silverware, with its use of gems and enamelling and the graceful wirework of its handles and finials. Here and elsewhere we can see how in the 1890s the rather severe Arts and Crafts style was yielding somewhat to the more decorative appeal of Art Nouveau.

The term Art Nouveau was coined in 1895 by Siegfried Bing, a German-born Parisian dealer. His shop in Paris was called La Maison de l'Art Nouveau, and he sold the work of British designers as well as that of Frenchmen Gaillard and Gallé. It was not long before Art Nouveau began to extend its influence over much of Europe. Indeed it also reached America, and is most memorably reflected in the products of Louis Comfort Tiffany who designed some very fine art metalwork in sterling silver and other metals, as well as his famous leaded-glass lampshades.

In Germany Kayser & Sons produced a range of fine metalware designed by Hugo Leven, under the brand name Kayserzinn. The Württembergische Metalwaren Fabrik (WMF) turned its production over almost entirely to the new *Jugendstil*, as Art Nouveau was called there. Its designs in pewter or nickel-silver, often with green glass liners, were increasingly elaborate and sometimes bordered on the kitsch.

In Italy the new style came to be called simply 'Il Stile Liberty' after Arthur Lazenby's London store, Liberty's. It was Liberty's that championed and popularized what in England in the 1890s was an extremely avant-garde style. Their chief metalware designer was the Manxman Archibald Knox.

DRESSER'S INFLUENCE

Knox arrived in London in the 1890s to work initially for Dr Christopher Dresser at his design studio in Barnes. Author of *Principles of Decorative Design*, Dresser was a seminal influence on many designers of the period, and his domestic metalware of the 1870s and 1880s anticipated modernist ideas by many years. Rex Silver, who designed for Liberty's, also worked for Dresser at one time.

At the end of the 1890s Knox began work for Liberty's on a range of silverware called 'Cymric', which was followed by pewterware called 'Tudric'. Heavily influenced by Celtic art, this was some of the best of British Art Nouveau, retaining much of the simplicity and geometry that Knox must have learned from Dresser, and combining it with the fluidity and rhythm of the French style.

Brass and Copper

It was the aim of the Arts and Crafts designers to elevate everyday objects to the status of art by applying new standards in design. W. A. S. Benson produced some silver-plated ware, but most of the production of his Hammersmith factory was given over to the manufacture of domestic objects in brass and copper.

His designs owed more to the modernist tendencies of Dr Christopher Dresser than to Art Nouveau. Benson's lamps, firescreens and light fittings are stark even by Arts and Crafts standards, though his kettles and teapots are nearer to the mainstream style of the Movement.

Benson sold his work at his own showroom in Bond Street as well as at Morris & Co. in Oxford Street and in Paris at Siegfried Bing's Maison de l'Art Nouveau. 'He preferred,' said his Times obituary, 'to approach his subject as an engineer rather than as a hand-worker; to produce beautiful forms by machinery on a commercial scale rather than single works of art.'

His influence was widespread in the Guilds, where many artefacts in brass and copper were produced by hand, though of course never as cheaply as by Benson's factory methods. Copper particularly appealed to the Arts and Crafts Movement for its lowly status, its inexpensiveness, its maleability and its beauty of colour and texture.

A gold-plated pewter table lamp with a fringed brass shade. The lamp dates from around 1900 and was made in Austria. The shade is more recent but is a close copy of the original.

PRICE GUIDE **8**

A seven-branch candleholder, made by W. A. S. Benson around 1900. A mass-produced piece in brass, it has holes for electric wires in the cups and has one replacement cup.

PRICE GUIDE **6**

PRICE GUIDE

▼ An English-made door fingerplate and matching handle, made in 1900. It is decorated with an Art Nouveau design of flowers. The fingerplate is from a set of 11.

PRICE GUIDE ❸

▶ A copper and brass kettle and muffin dish by W. A. S. Benson. It is one of his classic pieces and is beautifully made. It dates from the 1880s. Today it would make a fine decorative piece.

PRICE GUIDE ❼

▼ A two-branch brass and copper candlestick by W. A. S. Benson, made around 1905.

PRICE GUIDE ❻

◀ An electric table lamp shaped like an Aladdin's lamp. Made in brass and copper, it was produced in W. A. S. Benson's factory in 1906.

PRICE GUIDE ❻

Pewter, Silver and Silver-Plated Ware

Under the directorship of Carl Haegele, WMF in Germany produced some of the most outrageously curvilinear Art Nouveau metal-work ever made. It was variously described as the whip-lash style, the Spaghetti Style and, by Charles Rennie Mack-intosh, as 'resembling melted margarine'. The exuberance of their output, mostly in pewter or silver-plated ware, is never-theless hard to resist.

WMF's chief designer was Beyschlag, who seemed to relish pushing the style to its limits. Art Nouveau maidens appear everywhere, their hair winding on for ever, seamlessly entwined with stylized roots and foliage.

One has only to put a WMF frame, with its maiden and whiplash foliage, next to one by Mackintosh, with its austere elegance and cool geometry, to see the extraordinary breadth of design that the term Art Nouveau is used to cover. Both were made in pewter and at roughly the same time, but they are the product of radically different imaginations.

Between these two extremes lie many figural candlesticks and lamps in gilt bronze, electropla-ted pewter and white metal, as well as mirrors, sweetmeat dishes, caskets and jugs in solid silver or electroplated silver.

The style invaded every area of design and decoration, becoming a total look with which it was difficult to mix other styles. If you were serving tea in a William Hutton silver tea set, it had to be laid on a Guild of Handicraft silver tray, to which could be added a Liberty Cymric silver biscuit box and so on. The same effect could be achieved at less expense in pewter or electro-plated silver.

▼ *A highly decorated Art Nouveau sweet barrel, made by WMF at the turn of the century. It is in pewter and etched green glass, something of a WMF speciality.*

PRICE GUIDE ❼

▲ *A wall clock in pewter from Liberty's, made in 1905. At the turn of the century, Liberty's produced excellent pewter in their Tudric range, largely designed by Archibald Knox.*

PRICE GUIDE ❽

▲ *A single candlestick with three curving stems from a circular base. Made of pewter, it is one of Archibald Knox's Liberty designs.*

PRICE GUIDE ❻

PRICE GUIDE

◀ An elegant, tall decanter by WMF. Made of etched green glass and pewter, it has a hinged lid. It was produced in 1900.

PRICE GUIDE **8**

▶ A silver jug by Elkington, made in 1892. The crucifix on top of the lid suggests it may have been for church use.

PRICE GUIDE **6**

▼ A double sweet dish in pewter, with an Art Nouveau lady rising from the centre. It was produced by WMF at the turn of the century.

PRICE GUIDE **6**

▼ An unusual tureen in pewter. The lid, in the shape of an old helmet, has a particularly large, practical handle. Made in 1904, the tureen was designed by Archibald Knox for Liberty's.

PRICE GUIDE **6**

▼ A German-made easel mirror in polished pewter. Made around 1900, it is decorated asymmetrically, but with peacocks down each side.

PRICE GUIDE **8**

▶ An Edward VII coronation spoon in silver, with blue enamel decoration and Art Nouveau motifs. Part of Liberty's Cymric range, it was made in Birmingham in 1901.

PRICE GUIDE **6**

PRICE GUIDE

COLLECTOR'S TIPS

Art Nouveau is such a distinctive style that there is little problem for the collector in recognizing it. There was, however, a minor revival of interest in Art Nouveau in the 1930s, and reproduction metalwork was being made right up to the beginning of World War II. This was sometimes produced from the original moulds, so some care is needed, and particular attention should be paid to any hallmarks or touch marks.

Since the current trend for Art Nouveau began in the 1960s, there has been a good deal of reproduction, especially in the form of light fittings and lamps. These are not generally intended to deceive, and are, in many cases, of high quality, though of only passing interest to the true collector.

MAKERS' MARKS
The collector's life is greatly simplified by the fact that the main mass producers of art nouveau metalware, Liberty's and WMF, stamped all their work with their name. In addition, Liberty's pewter was stamped 'Tudric' and some of their silver, 'Cymric'. Most of Liberty's manufacturing was actually carried out in Birmingham, so the Birmingham hallmark will also appear on the silverware.

The same can be said for Tiffany's in New York, whose work was all stamped with the firm's logo and usually with the words: 'Tiffany Studios, New York'.

The specialist dealers in Art Nouveau will always carry examples of the art metalware which was such a feature of the period. Prices are rising all the time, but the would-be collector can always begin with some of the smaller, simpler items, say, of Liberty's pewter, which are still quite affordable.

The work of the Arts and Crafts Guilds is different because it was made by hand. The Guilds encouraged a consciously rough-hewn style complete with hammer-marks, and it is this that gives Arts and Crafts metalware its distinctive look. The objects were usually stamped with the Guild's mark – for instance, 'G. of H. Ltd' for Ashbee's Guild of Handicraft.

Expensive in their own time, these objects are now major collector's items tending to command higher prices than, say, Liberty's

Old and Repro
METAL PICTURE FRAMES WITH ART NOUVEAU DECORATION ARE STILL WIDELY MADE TODAY. THE FRAME AT LEFT SHOWS ITS AGE.

WMF Art Nouveau Pewter

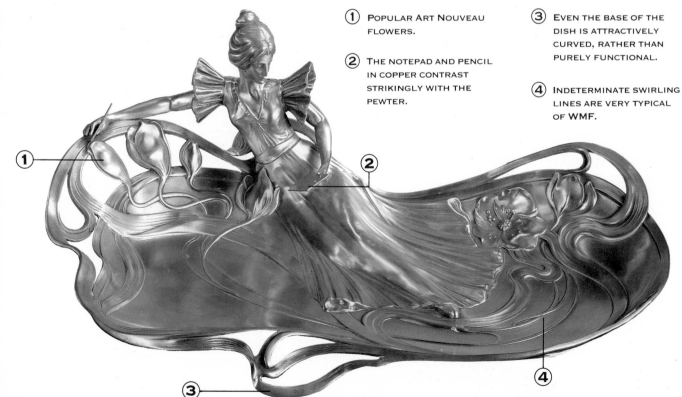

THIS ELABORATE PIECE IN ART NOUVEAU STYLE INCORPORATES MANY OF THE DECORATIVE FEATURES OF WMF'S WORK. THERE ARE NO STRAIGHT LINES, EVERYTHING IS CURVED. SWIRLING SPAGHETTI-LIKE LINES, WHICH IN THIS PIECE MIGHT EITHER BE RIPPLES IN THE WATER OR STRANDS OF WATER WEED (AND IN OTHER PIECES MIGHT BE LONG LOCKS OF HAIR), ARE VERY

TYPICAL OF WMF. HERE THE LINES ARE PICKED UP IN THE DESIGN OF THE HANDLES.

THE FLOWERS, ESPECIALLY THOSE ON THE LEFT, RECUR IN MANY ART NOUVEAU PIECES. THE LADY AT THE CENTRE, HERE HOLDING A NOTEPAD AND PEN, IS ANOTHER RECURRENT FEATURE, OF WMF METALWORK IN PARTICULAR.

THIS PEWTER DISH MIGHT HAVE BEEN USED PURELY DECORATIVELY OR TO HOLD SWEETS OR DELICACIES. IT WAS PRODUCED AROUND 1900.

GERMANY WAS VERY MUCH A CENTRE FOR ORNATE ART NOUVEAU METALWORK AND ALTHOUGH WMF, FOUNDED IN 1864, IS THE BEST KNOWN, THERE WERE MANY OTHER FIRMS.

① POPULAR ART NOUVEAU FLOWERS.

② THE NOTEPAD AND PENCIL IN COPPER CONTRAST STRIKINGLY WITH THE PEWTER.

③ EVEN THE BASE OF THE DISH IS ATTRACTIVELY CURVED, RATHER THAN PURELY FUNCTIONAL.

④ INDETERMINATE SWIRLING LINES ARE VERY TYPICAL OF WMF.

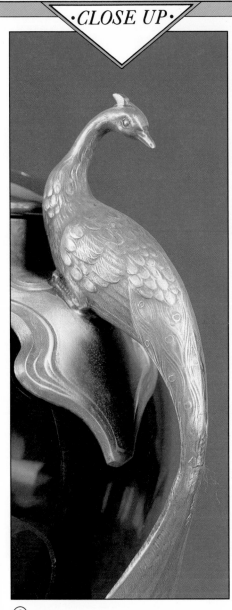

① PEACOCK HANDLE

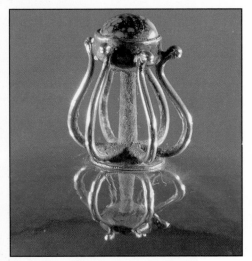

② WIREWORK FINIAL AND STONE

① THE PEACOCK WAS A GREAT FAVOURITE WITH ART NOUVEAU DESIGNERS. HERE ONE IS USED AS A HANDLE ON EITHER SIDE OF A GREEN GLASS SWEET BARREL.

② DELICATE WIREWORK IN SILVER, CAPPED BY A BLUE STONE. THESE DESIGN TOUCHES WERE A FEATURE OF C. R. ASHBEE'S WORK.

③ THE WMF STAMP CAN BE SEEN AT LEFT, NEXT TO AN EP MARK THAT INDICATES THE PIECE IS ELECTROPLATED.

④ READING FROM LEFT, LIBERTY'S (L & CO), MADE IN BIRMINGHAM (ANCHOR), IN SILVER (LION PASSANT), IN 1901 (B), IN THE CYMRIC RANGE.

⑤ EVEN THE HOT WATER PLUG ON THIS MUFFIN WARMER BY C. R. ASHBEE IS DECORATIVELY FINISHED.

⑥ W. A. S. BENSON'S STRAIGHTFORWARD STAMP, UNDER A COPPER FOOT.

③ WMF MARKS

④ LIBERTY'S CYMRIC MARKS

⑤ HOT WATER PLUG

⑥ ONE OF W. A. S. BENSON'S MARKS

metalware. In all cases, because of the intrinsic value of the metal, silver objects are more expensive than those in pewter or other base metals.

CLEANING TECHNIQUES

Silver can be cleaned using any of the usual polishes. When storing, wrap silver in a plastic bag – it will stay clean longer. Put a piece of camphor in the drawer or cupboard to keep it bright. Remember to wash table silver and cutlery to remove the chemicals before use.

When cleaning pewter, never use a metal cleaning powder or liquid as these may damage the surface. Stick to warm, soapy water and then dry and polish with a soft chamois or cloth. Bad stains may be removed by gently rubbing with the finest steel wool, dipped in olive oil – the oil will prevent scratching. To clean brass and copper, rub them with a cut raw lemon dipped in fine salt; or else use a mild polish.

Major restoration of antique pewter, silver or base metals should be carried out by specialists, though minor repairs to pewter, brass and copper can be done by soldering.

For the specialist collector there are many possible areas, such as Liberty's Art Nouveau, figural lamps, mirrors and picture frames. Silver or electroplated cutlery might be an interesting area – Mackintosh, Voysey and George Walton all produced designs in this period.

POINTS TO WATCH

■ When cleaning take care never to remove the patina on old metal objects, as

doing this will drastically reduce their value.

■ Don't store pewter in an oak cupboard, as oak gives off fumes which corrode the metal.

■ All silver must carry hallmarks by law. These are the maker's mark, the town mark (an anchor for Birmingham, a leopard's head for London), the silver mark itself (a lion passant) and a date letter.

▶ An electroplated soup tureen and ladle, designed by Christopher Dresser for Hukin & Heath. Though it looks modern it was designed in 1880. It was also made with ebony handles.

Pewter

Pewter has a rough-hewn quality that is very appealing. It underwent a revival in the late 19th century, led by Liberty's Tudric range

Pewter is an alloy of tin with other metals. Copper or lead are usually added to make the tin less brittle and easier to cast. Pewter has been used for domestic purposes since Roman times. Medieval craftsmen began using it for tableware, as a relatively cheap substitute for silver. In 1348 a trade guild, the Pewterers' Company, was founded in London to set standards of workmanship and to register craftsmen.

For 500 years, pewter was the metal of choice for everyday tableware, cutlery, drinking vessels, jugs, measures, vases and candlesticks. Easy to work, non-corrosible and in plentiful supply, pewter's only drawback was its inability to withstand great heat.

By 1700, three qualities of pewter were recognized by the Pewterers' Company, though there were no hard and fast rules about the proportions of metals used in the alloys. Hard metal, or plate pewter, was the best, with a high proportion of copper and maybe a little bismuth. It was used for plates, tankards and spoons and was generally worked by hammering pieces cut from a sheet. The next grade was trifle pewter, containing around one-fifth lead and antimony. It could be cast or turned, though it was often hammered as well to compact the metal. It was used for ale pots, funnels and candlesticks, as well as lesser quality spoons. The third quality, lay or ley pewter, had a 20-25 per cent lead content and was generally reserved for cruder wares and for vases, measures, inkwells, snuff-boxes and chamber pots.

In the 1790s, Britannia metal – 90 per cent tin, 8 per cent antimony and 2 per cent copper – was developed and soon replaced plate pewter for the best wares. It had a silver-white lustre that could be maintained by polishing and it could be die-stamped, cast or turned with equal ease, making it particularly suitable for factory production.

PEWTER MARKS

From 1503, all pewterers registered their personal touch marks with the Pewterers' Company. The marks were kept for reference on special touch plates at Pewterer's Hall. Early ones were destroyed in the Great Fire of London in 1666, but those made since are still extant. The marks were impressed, rather than engraved, on handles or on the rims of flatware. Marks were also registered at Edinburgh but London was the main centre. The system ceased to operate in the 1820s.

Originally, touch marks were likely to be simply sets of initials; later ones were more elaborate. They are the most reliable way of attributing and dating a piece of pewter, though if a date appears in the mark it is the date of registration rather than of manufacture.

Other marks can appear. An X or the word 'superfine' indicates best quality plate. A Rose and Crown was stamped on export wares, and came into general use for fine pieces after 1690. Marks in imitation of silver hallmarks crop up from time to time between 1600 and 1800. After the mid-1820s, all pieces intended as measures, including ale pots, were stamped with an official mark comprising the cypher of the sovereign, a local emblem and possibly a date code on some pieces.

Decoration was usually cast or embossed. From the Restoration onwards, pieces can be found decorated with wrigglework. The lines of wrigglework were drawn by tapping a blunt chisel while rocking it from side to side. Incised work was done by journeymen engravers after about 1700. The marks of the owner were often stamped or incised in pewter, perhaps in the form of three initials in a triangle, called a triad. These add value, especially where they go to prove provenance.

ARTS AND CRAFTS

Pewter fell out of favour in the 1830s and 1840s, only to undergo a revival at the end of the century. In the 1860s, groups of artists inspired by the works of John Ruskin and repelled by the dominance of the machine in Victorian life, promoted a return to craft-based values.

▲ The vast assortment of items produced in art nouveau pewter ware range from the purely practical to the utterly frivolous, and are still elegant enough to grace any collector's cabinet.

The Arts and Crafts Movement, as it became known, sought a marriage of the old ways with new technical possibilities. Craftsmen banded together in guilds, schools and workshops as a reaction to factories, and drew their decorative ideas and motifs from nature. It remained a strong undercurrent in British design and the decorative arts for some 40 years before its full flowering as a peculiarly British strain of Art Nouveau at the turn of the century. The London store, Liberty's, at that time the arbiter of fashionable, slightly avant-garde, middle-class taste, was in the vanguard of Art Nouveau.

Pewter was one of many crafts revived. Inspired by the fine decorative work – 'Art Pewter' – of the German firm Kayserzinn, Liberty's began to produce its own range of pewter, under the brand name Tudric, at the turn of the century. Liberty's operated a strict rule of secrecy about their designers, but much of the Tudric range was the work of a Manxman, Archibald Knox. Using the interlaced decoration that became popular in the wake of the Celtic Revival, in combination with the stylized natural motifs of Art Nouveau, Knox and Liberty's designed a range of pewter ware that is now extremely collectable. Most pieces were machine-made by the Birmingham firm of Haseler. Sometimes the marks of hand-hammering on pieces were applied by machine.

Functional, traditional pieces included tankards, spoons, tea sets and plates. Applied decoration was added to vases, trays, biscuit boxes, inkwells, candlesticks and even clocks. Panels of green or electric blue enamel, pieces of mother-of-pearl and copper were used decoratively. Some fruit-bowls, cups and vases were made of cut-out pewter lined with coloured – usually green – glass. Tudric pieces were marked with the brand name and/or Liberty's logo, or were sometimes stamped 'English Pewter' or 'Solkets'.

WHAT TO LOOK FOR

Generally, the older the pewter, the more it is sought after, with most interest in the 17th and 18th centuries. The lidded flagons and tankards of this period and the larger plate are highly valued. Much easier to find are the barrel-shaped late-Georgian tankards and Victorian ones with heavy lids and glass bottoms. All old pewter should have oxidized to a soft, natural sheen of grey; Britannia metal can keep its silver colour if polished regularly, but once lost it can never be regained, and mint condition 19th-century Britannia metal is hard to find.

Pieces of old pewter should be well-balanced and show good workmanship, with no sharp edges or newly polished seams. Hinges and edges should be worn, and there may be concentric rings on the base of a piece of holloware where it has been turned on a lathe.

PITFALLS

The collection of pewter is fraught with difficulty for the beginner. There was a vogue for reproduction pieces in the 1920s and many rarer items have been faked, particularly 17th-century tankards and candlesticks. Pieces can only be authentic if the touch marks, their placing, the style of the piece, the workmanship, weight, patina and feel all point to

about the same period. Touch marks themselves have been faked; make sure that they show the right amount of wear, with no sharp edges to them.

Some 60-year-old reproductions may well have acquired a reasonable patina, but very old pewter will show additional signs of wear. There should be microscopic pitting on the piece and perhaps marks of scouring. The naturally soft metal will have acquired dents and cuts in normal use. These effects can be duplicated by a washing with acid and rough treatment, so check that the wear is reasonable and the cuts consonant with normal use. Some old pieces may just show little or no signs of wear.

The collector of art nouveau pewter will have no such problems. All Liberty's pieces are marked, and the only other major manufacturers of the period, Connell and Company, never reached the same standard, although they did use some Liberty's designs. In decoration, they substituted ceramic inlays for the enamelled panels of genuine Liberty's work. Decorative pieces were also produced in quantity by the German factories, Kayserzinn and WMF, and in one-offs by artists such as Lalique.

▲ Art nouveau pewter ware was particularly popular in Britain and Germany. The chocolate pot (left), coffee pot (right) and tulip vases are all examples of Tudric ware and bear the interlaced Celtic motifs typical of this range. The figurine fruit dish is from WMF – a leading German manufacturer.

INDEX

INDEX

INDEX

PICTURE CREDITS

Asprey: 21(bc). Chris Barker: 141(tr). Stephen Bartholomew: 56-57(c), 58-59, 60-61, 63(tl,tc,tr,cl,c,cr). Steve Bisgrove: 44-45(c), 46-47, 48-49, 50(c,b),51, 132-133(c), 134-135, 136-137, 138, 139(tl,tc,tr,cr). Blaise Castle House Museum, Henbury: 44(bl). Bridgeman Art Library: 11(tl) The Tate Gallery, London, 14 Agnew & Son. 28-29(c), 56(bl) Victoria & Albert Museum, London, 62(b) City of Bristol Museum & Art Gallery, 63(br), 69(tr), 71(tl), 76(bl) Mallet & Son (Antiques), 76-77(t) Victoria & Albert Museum, London, 77(cr), 88(bl) S.J. Phillips, London, 97(tr), 105(tr), 111(br), 124, 139(br). Bristol City Museum & Art Gallery: 9(bc). Chatto & Windus Ltd: 128-129(c). Christie's Colour Library: 54, 55(tl,tr), 66-67(c), 80(bl), 104(bl), 132(bl). Christie's Geneva: 67(tr). Collection Viollet, Paris: 57(tr). Aubrey Dewar: 20(bl), 22-23, 24-25, 26, 27. The Dilettanti Society: 8-9. Ray Duns: 9(tr,cr,br), 10-11(c), 29(tr,cr,br), 30(br), 31, 77(tr,br), 78-79(b), 103(br), 112-113(c), 114, 115(tl,tr,c), 125(bl,br), 126(tr,cr), 126-127(b), 127(tr), 129(tr,cr,br), 130-131(b). Edimedia/R. Guillemot: 62(tl). Mary Evans Picture Library: 10(tr), 53(tr), 126(tl), 131(tr). Fine Art Photographic Library: 30(cl), 89(tr), 113(tr). Fotomas: 125(tr). Christine Hanscomb: 21(tr). Claus Hansmann: 65(tc,bc), 67(c). John Hollingshead: 12-13, 15(tr), 64-65(c), 66(tr), 80-81(c), 82-83, 84-85, 86, 87(tl,tc,tr,cl,c,cr), 104-105(b) Peter Christie of J. Christie and Victor Franses, 106-107 Peter Christie of J. Christie (pheasant), 108-109 Victor Franses Gallery (chinoise bust), 110(t), (b) Peter Christie of J. Christie, 111(tl,tc,tr,cl,c,cr). Angelo Hornak Library: 37(tr). Hulton Picture Company: 28(bl). Laurois-Giraudon/Malmaison: 45(tr). Ranald Mackechnie: 113(bc). Michael Michaels: 140(tr). The National Trust: 50(cl) Nick Carter, 81(tr) Nick Carter. Ian O'Leary: 16, 17, 18-19. Prudential Fine Art Auctioneers: 8(bl), 87(br). Peter Reilly: 74(bl). Ann Ronan Picture Library: 130(tl). Duncan Smith: 36(bl), 36-37(c), 38-39, 40-41, 42, 43, 116(bl), 116-117(b), 118-119, 120-121, 122, 123. Spink & Son Ltd: 97(br). Tate Gallery, London: 117(t). Gerry Tubby: 20-21(c). Victoria & Albert Museum, London: 15(cl), 129(bc). Rosemary Weller: 32-33, 34-35(t), 35(cr), 52-53(c), 68-69(c), 70, 71(tc), 72-73, 74-75(t), 75(tr), 88-89(c), 90-91, 92-93, 94, 95, 96, 98-99, 100-101, 102, 103(tl,tc,tr,cl,ucr,cr). Yale Center for British Art/Paul Mellon Collection: 78-79(t).